HORIZON

WINTER, 1976 · VOLUME XVIII, NUMBER 1

ᴄHoᴙizon

WINTER, 1976 • VOLUME XVIII, NUMBER 1

EDITOR
Shirley Tomkievicz

MANAGING EDITOR: James F. Fixx

ART DIRECTOR: Kenneth Munowitz

ARTICLES EDITORS: Kaethe Ellis, Priscilla Flood

SENIOR ASSOCIATE EDITOR: Mary Sherman Parsons

ASSOCIATE EDITOR: Linda S. Sykes

ASSISTANT EDITOR: Marya Dalrymple

EDITORIAL ASSISTANT: Arthur S. Hayes

CONTRIBUTING EDITORS: Walter Karp, Barbara Klaw

COPY EDITOR: Sarah Nichols Smith

ASSISTANT TO THE EDITOR: J. Muriel Vrotsos

ROVING EDITOR: Frederic V. Grunfeld

SENIOR EDITOR
Joseph J. Thorndike

ADVISORY BOARD

Gilbert Highet, *Chairman*, Frederick Burkhardt,
Charles L. Mee, Jr., John Pfeiffer, John Walker

EUROPEAN CONSULTING EDITOR: J. H. Plumb, *Christ's College, Cambridge*

CHIEF, EUROPEAN BUREAU: Gertrudis Feliu, *11 rue du Bouloi, 75001 Paris*

LONDON EDITOR: Christine Sutherland, *51 Victoria Road, London W8*

AMERICAN HERITAGE PUBLISHING COMPANY

PUBLISHER
Marjorie C. Dyer

EDITORIAL ART DIRECTOR
Murray Belsky

SENIOR EDITORS, HORIZON
Marshall B. Davidson, Oliver Jensen

HORIZON is published every three months by American Heritage Publishing Co., Inc. Editorial and executive offices: 1221 Avenue of the Americas, New York, N.Y. 10020. Secretary: William Cusick. All correspondence about subscriptions should be addressed to: HORIZON Subscription Office, 379 West Center St., Marion, Ohio 43302.

Single copies: $7.50. Subscriptions: $26.00 per year in the U.S.; Canada and elsewhere: $28.00.

Cumulative indexes for Volumes I–V, VI–X, and XI–XV are available at $7.50. HORIZON is also indexed in the *Readers' Guide to Periodical Literature*. The editors welcome contributions but can assume no responsibility for unsolicited material. Title registered U.S. Patent Office. Second-class postage paid at New York, N.Y., and at additional mailing offices.

"Here Comes a Candle to Light You to Bed, Here Comes a Chopper to Chop off Your Head"

" 'Shall I tell you why we have brought you here? To cure you! To make you sane! . . . We are not interested in those stupid crimes that you have committed. The Party is not interested in the overt act: the thought is all we care about. . . . We do not merely destroy our enemies; we change them.' He was bending over Winston. His faced looked enormous because of its nearness, and hideously ugly."

The year, of course, is 1984, the scene a room in the Ministry of Love. O'Brien, a bigwig in the Thought Police, is haranguing poor Winston, who is hooked up to the pain machine. *1984* is one of the truly chilling cautionary tales of our time, but hard to read in utter seriousness anymore—if only because its trappings have been borrowed so often by films of the "Now I have you in my clutches" variety.

And yet our fears of a totalitarian future controlled by mad scientists cannot quite be laid to rest. As Kenneth Lamott remarks in the lead article of this issue ("On Controlling Human Behavior"), it is distinctly possible that we are heading for a beehive society—an intolerable fate "for people who persist in thinking they are free." The nervous observer scanning the landscape for signs of encroaching beehive-ism might well ponder the doings of the National Institute of Mental Health. It is part of the Alcohol, Drug Abuse, and Mental Health Administration, which is part of the giant bureaucracy known as the Public Health Service, which in turn is part of the Department of Health, Education, and Welfare. Like O'Brien, NIMH is out not to destroy the mentally unsound but to change them. It wants to cure them. It wants to make them sane.

NIMH began operations in 1949, the same year, by coincidence, that *1984* appeared. Besides compiling statistics, publishing pamphlets, and in general behaving like a government agency, NIMH annually disposes of a hefty sum of public money. Last year its budget amounted to 430 million dollars, of which 92 million went into research and almost 200 million into community mental-health centers around the nation. No particular secret is made of any of this, and yet few Americans are even aware that NIMH exists.

The explorations into behavior modification that NIMH has financed range from "positive reinforcement" techniques (e.g., rewarding "good" behavior) to the use of psychoactive drugs, electroconvulsive therapies, and psychosurgery. Behavioral scientists have the ethical handicap—of which NIMH is well aware—of having to experiment on those with little say-so in the matter: pigeons, mice, chimpanzees, troublesome children, and the inmates of prisons and mental hospitals. In a recent pamphlet entitled "Behavior Modification," NIMH tries to set ethical standards for itself and its grantees. But did we really want or need a federal mental-health bureaucracy in the first place? And who are the mentally unhealthy?

Whatever ends it may pursue, NIMH is seldom in the public eye. A few years ago there was a minor to-do when Congressman Cornelius E. Gallagher of New Jersey denounced NIMH for giving a grant of 283,000 dollars to B. F. Skinner. (As Gallagher saw it, Skinner had used the money to live on while he wrote the best-selling *Beyond Freedom and Dignity*—and hardly qualified for public assistance anyway.) And in 1972, a Ralph Nader study group attacked the community mental-health centers as ineffectual and voiced concern about the "increasing vulnerability of American psychiatry to political and institutional manipulation."

Otherwise NIMH attracts small notice. Anyone who attacks it—or mental health as a worthwhile governmental goal—is usually looked upon as a kook. And how, indeed, is one to attack it? It is circumspect, scientific, and sane. It is above the fray. It sends no operatives around to administer drugs to prisoners or tranquilizers to "hyperactive" children. The research it finances is scientific and appears in the scientific journals. The ordinary people who pay for the whole procedure seldom have, or demand, the opportunity to scrutinize it.

The trouble with *1984* and *Brave New World* and *A Clockwork Orange* is that the beehive societies they depict came about, in each case, as the result of some cataclysm. The bomb falls, the bad guys come in, everything is changed. Before long, Orwell's "gorilla-faced guards" are on every street corner. The humanists, like Winston, have no choice but to surrender; O'Brien or his equivalent drags them off-stage.

But the cataclysm may not, in fact, arrive. If 1984 is just around the bend, it will probably not come in the form of mad scientists and brutal thugs. It will appear in some quite familiar garb, and we shall have no one to blame but ourselves. —S. T.

ITSUO ART MUSEUM, OSAKA

COVER: Aging and world-weary, the gifted despot Toyotomi Hideyoshi is the subject of this remarkably realistic portrait (reproduced in full at left) done around 1598, the year of his death. Beginning on page 12, Donald Keene describes the great period of Japanese history that Hideyoshi presided over. Accompanying the article is a portfolio of details from two six-panel screens that show life in Kyoto, Hideyoshi's capital city, in a day when it was more populous than Paris was.

On Controlling Human Behavior

Behavior modification by psychological methods may be
one of the great put-ons of our time.
But there are new developments that are faster, surer,
and bode no good whatsoever

The psychologist can hardly do anything without realizing that for him the acquisition of knowledge opens up the most terrifying prospects of controlling what people do and how they think and how they believe and how they feel.
                                    — J. ROBERT OPPENHEIMER

All men control and are controlled.
                                    — B. F. SKINNER

Although I didn't realize it at the time, I became involved in practicing behavior modification more than thirty years ago. Because I'd been born and reared in Japan and spoke the language fairly well, I spent a couple of war years interrogating Japanese prisoners of war, whose behavior I now recognize as having been shaped by the purest principles of applied behaviorist psychology.

At a stockade built on coral rock beyond the cane fields east of Pearl Harbor, my colleagues and I questioned the prisoners for strategic military purposes. Given the Japanese soldier's reputation for fierce loyalty to the emperor, it was not an undertaking that promised success. Against all odds, it worked.

Those warriors who had fought so tenaciously, those paragons of martial virtues, became meek and biddable citizens of our stockade. They turned into virtual fountains of information. On occasion they even volunteered to tell us everything they knew, if only an interrogator would pay attention to them.

If only an interrogator would pay attention to them—that turned out to be the key to shaping their extraordinary behavior. When a POW had had experiences that interested us, we called him back day after day to an interrogation cubicle, where we plied him with cigarettes, questioned him at length, and listened attentively. If the POW turned out to be a liar, stupid, or simply unco-operative, he was merely asked for the information required by the Geneva Convention—name, rank, and serial number—and sent back to the stockade. He was not abused, nor was his daily life changed in any way, except that when the prisoners were called out in the morning for questioning, he was left behind. The first time a rejected POW sent out word that he wanted to be interrogated again, we were surprised and amused. Later, we came to expect it.

Without knowing it, we had stumbled onto the principal discovery made by B. F. Skinner, the Godfather of behavior modification. This discovery (which Skinner announced in 1938 in *The Behavior of Organisms*) was that the behavior of animals, including man, can be influenced more effectively by immediate rewards—positive reinforcement—than it can by immediate punishment—negative reinforcement or, as it is also called, aversive conditioning.

From this seed have grown new branches of experimental psychology, learning theory, and psychotherapy. Behavior modification is a relatively new offshoot. It includes a variety of activities built around the thesis that by adjusting systems of rewards and punishments we can effectively control the behavior both of individuals and of people in groups. It is distinctively American in that it is characterized by a passion for results. It is also deliberately insensitive to the mental processes associated with obtaining these results.

In the thirty-eight years since his first book was published, Skinner has attained such an eminence that his name is often linked with that of the great Ivan Petrovich Pavlov, who discovered the conditioned reflex. Skinner looks on himself as the messiah of a new and better society based on his own principles of behavior. He is not, however, entirely happy with all of his followers. As we shall see, many behavior modifiers have fallen away from the simple and relatively humane principle of reward rather than punishment and have gone on to the headier pleasures of working with electrical impulses, the scalpel, ultrasonic vibrations, and chemicals that produce disagreeable effects.

No matter how unsympathetic I find Skinner as a moral philosopher and social planner (and I find him most decidedly so), I can only sympathize with him when he protests that his original doctrine has been corrupted and reminds his readers that the term "behavior modification" arose "in connection with the management of human behavior through contingencies of positive reinforcement specifically designed to replace the punitive techniques that are commonly observed in prisons and used by parents, teachers, employers, and others."

No matter how vigorously Skinner protests, the matter is now out of his hands. Dr. Bertram S. Brown, director of the National Institute of Mental Health, which puts about three million dollars a year into behavior modification research, includes aversive control among the acceptable techniques, but balks at control by electro-convulsive therapy, neurosurgery, or the "noncontingent" use of drugs. Others, such as the neurophysiologist Jose M. R. Delgado, see the salvation of mankind in perfecting ever more ingenious methods for the direct control of the brain by electrical impulses or surgery.

The net of behavior modification has been cast wide. Under the rubric of behavior modification, unruly prisoners are injected with a drug that makes them experience the sensations of drowning. College students are invited to join programs in which they will be painlessly cured of smoking or overeating. Convicted child molesters suffer electric shocks while looking at pictures of naked children. Other sex offenders are injected with Depo-provera, a drug that temporarily reduces the body's usable supply of male hormones. Critical bits of tissue are destroyed in the brains of young men prone to violence.

Behavior modification is clearly more than a fashionable new wrinkle among the applied psychologists, for it has focused our attention on questions that have obsessed moral and social philosophers since the Greeks. The central and unanswered question that remains is whether man is autonomous or an automaton. Furthermore, that philosophi-

PAVLOV   FREEMAN   SKINNER

Mixed modifiers: Ivan Pavlov discovered the conditioned reflex; Walter Freeman performed lobotomies with a golden ice pick; B. F. Skinner proposes human management by positive reinforcement.

cal question is complemented by a practical one: could a government intent upon extending its authority over the daily lives of its citizens accomplish its goals by using the technology of behavior modification?

We shall address ourselves to these questions first by looking into the history of behavior control through the centuries, then by exploring present-day applications of behavior modification. Finally we shall return to the central issues.

Only a god capable of seeing a person's entire structure of inner goals could establish contingencies for that person without creating conflicts that would lead to direct and violent confrontation.   —WILLIAM T. POWERS

• That we can read the history of civilization as the history of control has become a truism in the literature of behavior modification. Traditionally, parents control their children's behavior; those who own property control the behavior of those who don't; the employer controls his workers' behavior; the social group controls the behavior of the individual.

To consider a relatively benign example of pre-Skinnerian behavior modification, let us look at our urban public schools around the year 1900. Our tendency to sentimentalize the melting pot obscures the fact that what was going on in those schools was not only instruction in the three R's but also a mass effort at behavior modification that called for the "extinguishing" of behavior appropriate to the ghettos and *shtetlach* of Eastern Europe and the "shaping" of behavior appropriate to the Anglo-Saxon

culture of the New World.

The goal of turning immigrant Jewish children into little Americans seems so well-intended that we wonder for a moment where on earth the evil could have been. In fact, however, immigrant parents and native Americans who did not share the goals of the dominant system angrily denounced the schools as agents of enforced cultural assimilation. In St. Louis parents forced the public schools to use and teach German in the classrooms, and in 1917 there were riots in New York against new fashions of the assimilationist classrooms.

Throughout the ages, perhaps the closest approximation to behavior modification as we know it today has been the training of military or naval recruits, be they Spartan hoplites or Green Berets. Systems of recruit training have always had in common the objective of extinguishing civilian behavior and shaping the behavior required of a soldier or seaman. Although these systems have been created empirically rather than scientifically, they share with Skinner's doctrine a close analysis of desired and undesired behavior and a schedule of immediate reinforcement.

Furthermore, military training shares with behavior modification the problem of goals. As William T. Powers, a penetrating critic of Skinner's thought, has pointed out:

In order to control another person, one must establish contingencies or schedules of reinforcement. Whatever one chooses to use as a reward, he must make sure (i) that the subject needs or wants the reward and (ii) that the *only* way the subject can obtain the reward is by doing what the experimenter wants to perceive him doing.

With volunteers, the military has always done pretty well, for the recruits share their drill instructors' goals. When goals are not shared, the system turns out a proportion of Good Soldier Schweiks, Captain Yossarians, or deserters to Canada. Our experience of life leads us to expect that the most rigorously

constructed system of behavior modification will do the same.

There are four main points to this excursion into history. The first is that there is much about behavior modification that isn't new. The second is that all behavior modification is learning, and all learning that has observable consequences is behavior modification. The third is that techniques devised to modify behavior have always worked best when practical results are demanded in a hurry and when a concern for the integrity of the individual is at a minimum. The fourth is the suspicion that there are built-in reasons why behavior modification doesn't necessarily work.

---

362. Behavior Modification (4)

Basic processes of reinforcement, operant and classical conditioning, and social learning. Analysis and modification of behavior through methods based on these concepts. Each student will carry out a behavior modification project on himself or another person.

—BULLETIN OF SONOMA STATE COLLEGE, CALIFORNIA

● The vast flow of words that poured through the public prints after the publication in 1971 of Skinner's *Beyond Freedom and Dignity* had its origins in the animal experiments he carried out at Harvard in the early 1930's. As a scientist, he made his lasting contribution with his earlier books, *The Behavior of Organisms* and *Science and Human Behavior* (1953), in which he demonstrated that rats and pigeons could, by a learning process he called "operant conditioning," be trained to perform actions that do not come to them naturally.

The fulcrum of operant conditioning is the connection between behavior and its immediate consequences. Skinner has explained how he taught pigeons to march in figure eights:

I watch a hungry pigeon carefully. When he makes a slight clockwise turn, he's instantly rewarded for it. After he eats, he immediately tries it again. Then I wait for more of a turn and reinforce again. Within two or three minutes, I can get any pigeon to make a full

A competitive Skinnerian pigeon hits a cross-court drive to an opponent. The birds are caged—in the event a sore loser gets rough.

circle. Next I reinforce only when he moves in the other direction. Then I wait until he does both, and reinforce him again and again until it becomes a kind of drill. Within ten to fifteen minutes, the pigeon will be doing a perfect figure eight.

By similar means, Skinner has taught pairs of pigeons to play Ping-Pong, and anybody who has seen the films of this remarkable performance will give Skinner full marks as a pigeon trainer. Yet for centuries clever people have trained animals to perform ingenious tricks. The solid contribution Skinner has made to psychology is not the discovery that animals can be trained by rewards alone, but an experimentally verified description of the process of learning by operant conditioning.

Sometime in the early 1950's Skinner's vision passed from rats and pigeons to people, and since then he has functioned more as a publicist than as a scientist. It is significant that the first

Dr. Jose Delgado, neurosurgeon and stuntman, halts a charging bull with an impulse to an electrode implanted in the animal's brain.

sentence of his most recent book, *About Behaviorism*, published in 1974, describes behaviorism as a philosophy rather than a science. The foundation of Skinner's standing as a utopian novelist and as a social philosopher is the argument that if pigeons can be taught to play Ping-Pong by operant conditioning, human beings can be taught by similar methods to follow patterns of behavior chosen by their trainer. Yet, paradoxically, the subjects will remain unaware of the high degree of control to which they are responding. As Skinner phrased it:

We can achieve a sort of control under which the controlled, though they are following a code much more scrupulously than was ever the case under the old system, nevertheless *feel free*. They are doing what they want to do. …That's the source of the tremendous power of positive reinforcement—there's no restraint and no revolt. By a careful cultural design, we control not the final behavior, but the *inclination* to behave. …

The flood of literature that has been produced in recent years by writers both sympathetic to and opposed to behavior modification has worked to obscure the plain fact that this thesis runs counter to our common experience of life and has received only the most tenuous support from the actual performance of behavior modification in the real world.

Behavior modification's real-world claims appear to be strongest where psychotherapy is concerned. This often takes a highly structured form in which the goals shared by the therapist and his client are spelled out in a "contract." A woman who wishes to quit smoking might, for example, contract to reduce her consumption until she reaches the point of no consumption at all. The therapist will require her to keep a chart of the number of cigarettes she smokes each day, the declining line acting as positive reinforcement. He might also establish increasingly restrictive conditions on when and where she can light up, until in the end it presumably becomes just too much bother.

There is no threat here. The threat lies in the possibility that behavior modification may be used for the control of people who are unconscious of being manipulated in the pursuit of goals set by somebody else—a government, for example. The balance of the evidence is that Skinner's principles of operant conditioning have not yet been made to work in any but the most trivial human situations or in the most marginal and highly controlled environments. Where these principles have worked, the success has been accidental rather than essential and is not necessarily repeatable, which is to say it is not scientific.

It is just possible that behavior modification by psychological means is one of the great put-ons of our time. I wish I could believe that, but, whatever the case, I fear that much mischief remains to be done in its name. For impatient younger psychologists are developing methods that are faster and surer and seem to be carried on to no good end.

Give me a no-nonsense down-to-earth behaviorist, a few drugs and simple electrical appliances, and in six months I will have him reciting the Athanasian Creed. —W. H. AUDEN

"Stop it, stop it, stop it," I kept on creeching out. "Turn it off you grahzny bastards, for I can stand no more." It was the next day, brothers, and I had truly done my best morning and afternoon to play it their way and sit like a horrorshow smiling malchick in the chair of torture while they flashed nasty bits of ultraviolence on the screen, my glazzies clipped open to viddy all, my plott and rookers and nogas fixed to the chair so I could not get away.

—ANTHONY BURGESS, *A Clockwork Orange*

• One does not have to share Auden's sardonic vision or the neogothic fantasies of *A Clockwork Orange* to enter a world that is repellent beyond ordinary imagining. The literature of behavior modification abounds with self-congratulatory accounts of difficult successes achieved through methods and chemicals that are as remarkable for their power to disgust as for their ingenuity. None of this, of course, is en-

"Boy, have I got this guy conditioned! Every time I press the bar down, he drops in a piece of food."
—The Columbia University Jester

tirely new. It is recorded, for example, that Pliny the Elder recommended placing spiders in an alcoholic's wine. Nor is the use of nauseating or pain-producing substances to control behavior particularly new or particularly scientific. Consider the threat of a dose of castor oil to control fractious children.

We must, however, make something of a moral leap from methods such as these, however deplorable they may have been, to sanctioning in the name of scientific behavior modification the use of powerful drugs that cause great suffering. Dr. Bertram Brown observes with distaste that drugs such as Antabuse (for alcoholism) and Anectine (which produces the sensations of death through drowning) have "been seriously misused, especially in prison settings, where they are given to persons in retribution for real or imagined lack of 'cooperation' on their part, or as a way of keeping recalcitrant persons 'in line.' The noncontingent use of drugs lies outside the purview of behavior modification." It is a revealing comment, for it leaves the "contingent" use of drugs—that is, their use as a reward or punishment contingent on behavior—inside what is considered the proper "purview" of behavior modification.

One cannot think for very long about the use of drugs in controlling behavior without being reminded that the literature of every civilized race is full of references to such substances as soma, wine, hashish, opium, bhang, sacred mushrooms, and the fabled lotus that made Ulysses and his shipmates unmindful of their homes. Nor is history innocent of the encouragement of drug use as a means of controlling the behavior of entire populations.

To my mind, the most dishonorable example of this was the infliction of

alcohol on the North American Indians. Alcohol came down the St. Lawrence with the seventeenth-century French fur-traders, the *voyageurs*. Entire nations were destroyed, notably the Illinois, the largest tribe of the central prairies, who, sodden with alcohol, were wiped out by the Iroquois.

The white man was not responsible for the Indians' weakness for alcohol, but he was most certainly responsible for encouraging and profiting from it. There is not so great a difference as one might imagine, in principle at least, between the chemical control of the Indian and the chemical control of present-day groups who are considered to be deviant from the mainstream. Black activists, for example, have charged that the heroin epidemic has been encouraged in order to emasculate young black males socially and politically. And amphetamines, which usually act as stimulants, are also used as sedatives to quiet "hyperactive" schoolchildren, whose symptoms include noisiness and short attention spans.

Although there is no common agreement on the behavior that constitutes mental illness, we have in the past found it practical to lock up substantial numbers of people because their behavior is dangerous, distracting, or annoying to the rest of us. The theory has been that the behavior of the patient will be modified in a hospital by psychiatrists, clinical psychologists, and other professionals and subprofessionals skilled in the behavioral sciences.

This, of course, has been part of the trouble. People skilled in the behavioral sciences tend to share a behaviorist view of man. I cherish a professional report I read a number of years ago in a scientific journal. The report describes the experiences of a group of volunteers, including a psychologist and a psychiatrist, who got themselves committed to mental hospitals in order to observe the inner workings of these asylums. The volunteers at first felt obliged to record their observations in secret, hiding in a corner of a latrine or crouching in bed. Soon they discovered it didn't make any difference. The other inmates had already figured out that they were reporters of some sort; the staff, from psychiatrists to orderlies, *knew* that they were crazy.

The pseudo-patients began boldly writing their notes while sitting comfortably at tables in the dayroom. As the report put it, "If no questions were asked of the pseudo-patients, how was their writing interpreted? Nursing records for three patients indicate that the writing was seen as an aspect of their pathological behavior. 'Patient engages in writing behavior' was the daily nursing comment on one of the pseudo-patients who was never questioned about his writing."

Patient engages in writing behavior! At one stroke an extraordinarily complex mental process has been reduced to its observable consequences, the frequent manipulation of a writing instrument on paper. It is the epitome of what Arthur Koestler has called "ratomorphic psychology."

And it is not unrelated to what has been going on with "emotionally disturbed" people both in and out of mental hospitals during the past years. The doctrine appears to be, *If a person's behavior seems queer, give him a drug.* If he writes compulsively, stupefy him and he will stop; never mind why he was writing.

The use of drugs to modify behavior poses practical and moral questions that do not yield easily. If we are concerned only with outward behavior as it is seen by a behaviorist, the widespread use of drugs can be considered an unqualified blessing insofar as it frees disturbed people from strait jackets or life in the snake pit. If this were all, the verdict would be clear.

• I recently toured a new and quite grand psychology building at a midwestern university. My guide was the head of the department, a man with a wry and pleasant manner. He took me down into the basement to admire the laboratories.

In one room, I joined a pair of graduate students who were watching a television monitor that showed a pigeon in the experimental device known as a Skinner box. On the screen, the pigeon went peck-peck-peck. The students' heads went up-down up-down up-down. In an adjoining room lights went blink-blink-blink on the display console of the electronic boxes that recorded the pigeon's performance. Nobody was recording the students' performance, which I thought equally remarkable.

The next laboratory held several aquariums housing small gray fish about the size of dime-store goldfish. I asked my guide what they were being used for. He told me that students had done prefrontal lobotomies on them. I asked what effects had been observed. "Well," he answered, looking owlish, "if I recall correctly, their capacity to learn has been somewhat diminished."

If the current bitter controversy was merely over the use of psychosurgery to relieve the epileptic of his convulsions, the depressed patient of his self-destruc-

A backsliding member of a smoking clinic learns the power of negative reinforcement.

tive impulses, or the terminal cancer patient of intractable and unimaginable pain, the verdict would be clear here also. Yet psychosurgery has also been used to change the behavior of people who are merely troublesome to the rest of us. Although the subjects are human beings rather than fish, their mental capacities also appear to be somewhat diminished after the procedure.

Psychosurgery in the present use of the word goes back to the 1930's, when a Portuguese neurologist, Antonio C. Egas Moniz, invented the prefrontal lobotomy, which in experiments with monkeys had been found to have a subduing effect on the behavior of individuals who tended to be overexcited, aggressive, and violent. Lobotomies caught on in the United States, where they enjoyed a vogue during the 1940's, particularly in mental institutions and prisons.

The leading American lobotomist, Dr. Walter Freeman, is said to have arrived at the operating room carrying a gold ice pick in a velvet-lined box. Rather than cutting into the skull above the temple, as the Portuguese did, Freeman drove the ice pick through the eye socket and into the brain, severing the fibers between the thalamus and the frontal lobe. Behavior did indeed change, but not always predictably. Critics of Freeman told the story of the peeping Tom who, having been lobotomized, no longer slunk around back yards and alleyways but walked boldly up to bedroom windows.

Lobotomies went out of style in the 1950's, because new drugs and electroshock were found to have much the same effects with much less trouble. Also, their effects were reversible.

The present practice of psychosurgery calls for destroying tiny portions of the brain by scalpel, ultrasound, electric currents, or freezing. The surgeon's target areas are the cingulate gyrus (for anxiety, depression, or intractable pain), the thalamus (for violent behavior, and the amygdala (for epilepsy or violent behavior). The best current estimate is that fewer than a thousand psychosurgical operations are included among the approximately forty thousand brain operations performed in the United States each year.

The issues at stake here have been clouded rather than clarified by some of the more intransigent opponents of psychosurgery. Yet if, God forbid, one of my children was to suffer from epilepsy or intractable pain, I would find it hard to deny him relief if I was convinced that the odds were in his favor. The real issue, it seems to me, is the practice of psychosurgery to modify the behavior of mental patients and prisoners who cannot be presumed to have freely given their informed consent.

The issue of psychosurgery is further confused by the pronouncements of scientists like Dr. Jose Delgado, who has made himself the messiah of a New Jerusalem to be achieved through electrical control of the brain. Dr. Delgado has enraged his enemies and embarrassed some of his colleagues by his showmanship. In his best-remembered performance, he entered the ring with a bull in whose brain he had implanted radio-controlled electrodes. The bull snorted, pawed the ground, and took aim at the medical school professor. Delgado held his ground with the confidence of Manolete. The bull charged. Delgado flipped a switch on a miniature radio transmitter and—lo!—the bull lumbered to a halt and turned away. It was a virtuoso performance.

Delgado has also implanted electrodes in the brains of monkeys and people. He can thereby control the behavior of the subject, obliging one unfortunate monkey, for example, to go through the same sequence of actions twenty thousand times. He can cause a human subject to make a fist or turn his head to one side. (When he begins, however, he cannot predict what the resulting action will be.) Perhaps the most disturbing aspect of these experiments is that the human subject always considered the action spontaneous and offered

Delgado a "reasonable" explanation for it: "I am restless," or "I heard a noise." So much for freedom of the will, we can hear somebody say.

Delgado has left his laboratory at the Yale Medical School and is back in his native Spain, pursuing his goal of "conquering the mind." He is a gifted experimentalist, is in love with his tools, and is working toward the goal of a "cerebral pacemaker" small enough to be implanted entirely inside the skull. Any person so equipped would truly be a predictable man.

To hope that the power which is being made available by the behavioral sciences will be exercised by the scientists, or by a benevolent group, seems to me a hope little supported by either recent or distant history.   —CARL ROGERS

When science develops techniques that have the potential to fundamentally change society, society has the right to determine how the technique is to be used, whether it should be developed in the first place, and if so, under what constraints.   —SENATOR EDWARD KENNEDY

• As we have seen, the social and moral problems represented by the behavior modification movement—and it *is* a movement, complete with bumper stickers, THINK BEHAVIOR—are extraordinarily complex. At the center of the nest of problems is the question of whether or not new techniques are being developed that will make possible the control of mass populations.

Given the inherent costliness of psychosurgery, it does not seem at all

likely that millions of people will ever be equipped with Dr. Delgado's microminiaturized control units. It is possible, though, that one day we will learn enough about the precise functioning of the brain to equip a selected group of people, numbering in the hundreds or thousands, with computerized cerebral implant circuitry that will give them intellectual powers greater than the rest of us as well as the will to control us, which could thereby create a new ruling elite.

No convincing evidence exists that anybody has been able to use Skinner's techniques of reinforcement to manipulate the behavior of large numbers of people in any way that represents an advance over the age-old techniques of behavior control in the schoolroom or before the ballot box. Perhaps, however, we are merely awaiting the practical genius who will cut through Skinner's doughy and pretentious prose, seize upon the essential principles, and brilliantly put them to work in the pursuit of social or political goals.

It may not be entirely a coincidence that during the same years in which Skinner has been publicizing behavior modification, a revolution has taken place involving the mass modification of behavior on a scale that the world has never seen before. I refer of course to the Chinese Revolution.

Whether or not we think the Chinese Revolution a bright promise or a nightmare, we are obliged to recognize that during the past twenty-five years a deliberately designed program of behavior modification has affected more people than ever before in the world's history. The means that have been used have been pragmatic, nonscientific, ideologic, goal-oriented, and sometimes brutal. But clearly, Mao Tse-tung and not B. F. Skinner will go down in history as the leading behaviorist of our time.

For us in the Western world, a behavioral revolution as pervasive as China's is fortunately still the raw material of the fiction writer. Yet I do not think it

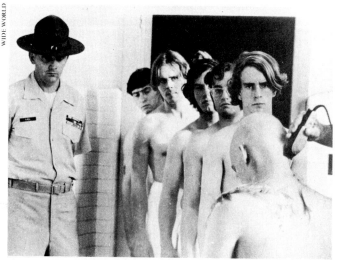

Apprehensive Marine recruits are about to be shorn of their nonregulation locks—a traditional behaviorist device in boot camp.

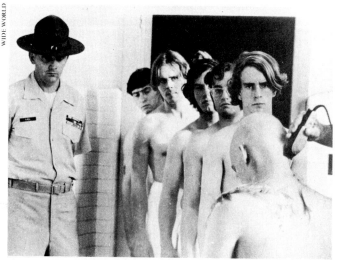WIDE WORLD

is too early to call a halt, even a temporary one, to the development of the technology of behavior modification.

As we have seen, it is extraordinarily difficult to assess the point at which scientific behavior modification has arrived and where it is likely to go. It would be comforting to conclude that behavior modification is no real threat because Skinner is largely a paper tiger and Delgado is the prototype of the mad scientist. Both of these strike me as reasonable propositions, but we have little sense of the direction in which the technology of behavior is being pushed by men and women working in other laboratories throughout the world or of what their ultimate goals may be. There is only the sense that things are moving too fast and that soon they may have gone too far.

It is time to stop work and take stock —and not just within the community of behavioral scientists but with the active participation of such representatives of the public interest as philosophers, politicians, and even poets. The issues to be weighed go far beyond the scientific and technical issues, for the problems raised by behavior modification are both practical and moral—practical in that behaviorism embodies some powerful principles of learning, and moral in that it touches directly on our conviction of individual freedom.

I have in a small way been an orthodox behaviorist myself. Years ago, when I had first been exposed to Skinner's learning theory, I invented a behaviorist game to teach one of my sons the multiplication table, using a deck of playing cards to generate the problems, and pennies as positive reinforcement for correct answers. Although John had wrestled unsuccessfully with the multiplication table at school for several weeks, he had it pat within an hour.

This, it seems to me, is the only sort of learning to which behaviorism can properly contribute. Using a toilet at the proper time, driving a car safely, correctly recognizing shapes and letters and numbers and words and their various combinations and permutations, learn-

Chairman Mao may be the ultimate behaviorist. These farm laborers are well launched on the path to a "socialist consciousness."

ing, in other words, that calls for mastering elementary social behavior and physical skills and absorbing a basic body of information—here behaviorism is on its proper turf.

Learning to be a decent human being is something else entirely. It would have been an act of overweening arrogance on my part to have tried to teach John to be truthful and kind and loyal by some extension of the cards and the pennies. Furthermore, it would have been based on a view of human nature that is not only contrary to my experience of life but abhorrent to me as well. As the literature of the world testifies, one of the glories of the human race is the infinite variety in which men and women are shaped and the unpredictability of their behavior.

When coming to grips with the behavior of a real human being, the behaviorist has demonstrated that he can chip away quite effectively at the corners but that he cannot permanently change the essentials without drugs, surgery, or an intensity of effort that is far out of proportion to the desired results. In this sense, behavior modification as it is practiced is, in its own terms, uneconomic. More damningly in the eyes of a humanist critic, it has no place in its contingencies and schedules of reinforcement for the internal wellsprings of our

most significant actions. As Edgar Z. Friedenberg has put it, behavior modification "offers itself as an inauthentic substitute for love and will, and hence is essentially frivolous about existence."

This is why I fear behaviorism as a principle of social organization. As we have become nervously aware during the past quarter-century, the world is changing both irreversibly and at an accelerated rate. We know from history that changes of this order of magnitude are, for better or worse, accompanied by changes in the social order.

If we are heading toward a beehive society, which seems to me a distinct possibility, it will, I think, come in the name of good rather than evil, and will be in pursuit of goals on which we are generally agreed. Given a consensus on goals, the pseudoscience of behavior modification offers a rough-and-ready technology of control that is well-fitted to the needs of a government intent on extending its authority ever more widely over the behavior of its citizens. The balance of the evidence is that behavior modification (short of drugs and surgery) can't destroy the essential integrity of the human being, but that it can help make the world an intolerable place for people who persist in thinking they are free.

The passage of two decades has only served to sharpen the heartfelt message that Robert Oppenheimer took to the American Psychological Association in 1955, when he declared that the nuclear scientists' pleas that their discoveries be used for the good of humanity "will seem rather trivial compared to those pleas which you will have to make and for which you will have to be responsible."

It is surely time to remind the behavioral scientists of that responsibility. The enterprises upon which they are engaged seem, at best, to promise mischief, and, at worst, to nourish the seeds of a great disaster.

Kenneth Lamott is a novelist who frequently writes about current affairs. His latest HORIZON article was "Is Prison Obsolete?" in the Summer, 1975, issue.

THE MAN WHO PUT JAPAN TOGETHER

Four centuries ago, Toyotomi Hideyoshi,

a rough-and-ready soldier,

distinguished himself as an actor, poet,

and patron of the arts.

He also turned a chaotic land into a nation

This portrait of Toyotomi Hideyoshi in formal attire was probably painted a short time after his death in 1598.

...otomi Hideyoshi was born in 1536, ...Year of the Monkey. As a child he ...known as "Little Monkey," and in ...portrait opposite he does have a ...iously simian look. But there was ...hing monkeylike about him. In his ...from humble origins to absolute ...ver, his success in uniting his coun-...and the brilliant flowering of the arts ...ier his lavish patronage, Hideyoshi ...y well be the most extraordinary po-...al figure in Japanese history. He set ...tone for the entire country during ...of its most momentous and creative ...s, the end of the sixteenth century.

...hortly before Hideyoshi's birth, his ...ier left a farm near what is now ...goya to take up arms for the local ...lord, Oda Nobuhide. During a long ...iod of incessant warfare, which had ...un in 1467 and would last more than ...undred years, the government in ...oto—both the civil authority headed ...he emperor and the military author-...represented by the shogun—was un-...e to take control. The warlords, not ...tent with seizing easily captured ...ds that belonged to the crown and the ...ility, tried to enlarge their holdings ...attacking their neighbors. The end-...destruction caused untold hard-...ps, but for ambitious young men like ...deyoshi it offered exceptional oppor-...ities to rise in the world.

...Ie made up his mind early in life that ...would be a warrior. After roaming ...und the country as a soldier of for-...e for some years, he joined forces ...h Oda Nobunaga, the son of the man ...father had served. Nobunaga ...ckly recognized the young man's tal-...s and raised him to officer's rank. In ...years of fighting that followed, ...deyoshi distinguished himself so con-...cuously that Nobunaga repeatedly ...omoted him. Nobunaga's forces ...zed larger and larger areas of the ...intry, and Hideyoshi won brilliant ...tories in many distant places. After a ...itury of complete disintegration, it ...med Japan would at last be unified.

...n 1582, however, a subordinate of ...bunaga's, Akechi Mitsuhide, treach-...usly attacked and killed the warlord

in Kyoto. Hearing the news on the field of battle, Hideyoshi hastily signed an armistice and rushed back to the capital. Twenty-one days after Nobunaga's death, Hideyoshi killed Mitsuhide. This triumph convinced Hideyoshi that he had the right to be acknowledged as Nobunaga's successor, and he successfully waged war upon everyone who disputed this right, including several of Nobunaga's sons.

As Hideyoshi's power grew, he acquired land, a wife, and various concubines, as well as a taste for upperclass luxuries. He also began to dream of founding a dynasty of military rulers: in 1583 he wrote to a thirteen-year-old girl, apparently one of his concubines, expressing his determination to establish a new order in Japan, one that would last fifty years.

Later that year, as the first step toward his new order, he started building a massive castle in Osaka to serve as the focal point of his rule, replacing the old capital in Kyoto. Earlier Japanese castles had been built mainly on hilltops and other easily defended sites, but Hideyoshi chose Osaka because of its accessibility to land and sea routes, the keys to trade. His castle was lavishly decorated, as we know from accounts by European visitors who gazed in wonder at the golden roof tiles, the ceilings and pillars covered with gold leaf, the magnificent wall paintings, and the spacious gardens. Though he later moved to Kyoto, Osaka Castle remained the center of his military power.

Hideyoshi now continued his victorious campaign of unification. The greatest obstacle to his plans was Tokugawa Ieyasu, another former lieutenant of Nobunaga's. After their forces fought an inconclusive battle in 1584, Hideyoshi changed his tactics: he decided to improve his relations with Ieyasu by offering his younger sister in marriage. The sister, as it happened, was already married, but Hideyoshi summarily resolved that problem by obtaining a divorce for her, and she became Ieyasu's

wife. Soon afterward Hideyoshi invited Ieyasu to visit his castle in Osaka, sending his own mother to Ieyasu's headquarters as a hostage and thus guaranteeing that Ieyasu would not be harmed. The plan worked: in 1585, Ieyasu swore allegiance to Hideyoshi, who set about conquering the rest of Japan.

In quick order he subdued enemy forces on the southern island of Kyushu, in the eastern part of the main island, and finally, in 1587, at the northern end of the main island. He had completed Nobunaga's work and unified Japan. In the meantime, he had also consolidated his position in Kyoto by being appointed to progressively higher court offices. He finally rose to *kampaku*, or chancellor, second only to the emperor. It was unheard of for a commoner to rise to the chancellorship, previously held only by members of the high-ranking Fujiwara family. When some of the Fujiwaras protested this violation of their ancient privileges, Hideyoshi had himself adopted by an elderly Fujiwara and took the family name.

Despite his military power, Hideyoshi never considered seizing the throne. But his vast financial resources and his position as chancellor immediately benefited the imperial court in Kyoto. For centuries the emperors of Japan had endured poverty and sometimes even real hardships. Often the imperial family earned a living by selling samples of their penmanship to visiting warlords; one emperor even lay unburied for months because there was not enough money to pay his funeral expenses. Hideyoshi's generosity enabled the imperial family once more to live in comfort. No doubt it flattered his vanity to think that the emperor and nobles were dependent on a farmer's son.

In 1587 Hideyoshi's palace in Kyoto, the Jurakudai, or Mansion of Pleasures, was completed, and the next year he invited the recently crowned emperor Go-Yozei to visit him there. The emperor's five-day visit was an occasion of pageantry and splendor. At its climax the dignitaries present signed a document binding themselves and their descen-

Suits of hinged samurai armor like the formidable one above were made obsolete by muskets in Hideyoshi's time.

dants to the protection of the estates of the emperor and the members of his court, and vowed to obey Hideyoshi's every command.

Hideyoshi strengthened the economic base for his manifold operations by seizing lands all over Japan and by placing the gold and silver mines directly under his control. The mines alone provided him with a vast annual income—forty-four hundred pieces of gold and eighty-nine thousand pieces of silver. So great was his wealth that in 1589 he distributed money to the assembled court nobles and military barons. In his castles and his Mansion of Pleasures he used gold and silver lavishly. He even had a portable gold teahouse, which he took with him wherever he went.

Hideyoshi was determined to wipe out resistance to his grandiose plans. To control farmers and small landowners—and prevent them from rising to power as he himself had done—he formulated repressive land codes and organized a survey assessing all land in terms of productivity. This measure was bitterly resisted by the peasants, as was his famous "sword hunt" of 1588, in which he confiscated all weapons—including swords, armor, spears, and bows and arrows. The farmers were told that the metal obtained by melting down their weapons would be used to cast a Great Image of Buddha for the city of Kyoto, thus guaranteeing their welfare in the afterlife, if not the current one.

Another element in Japan that presented a possible danger to Hideyoshi's rule was the foreigners. The first Europeans to reach Japan were Portuguese sailors whose ship had been blown off course in 1543. Six years later Francis Xavier, a founder of the Jesuits, landed in the southernmost part of Kyushu and began to preach Christianity with considerable success. The Christian missionaries were warmly welcomed by some barons, not only for religious reasons, but because of the possibilities of trade with the foreigners.

Oda Nobunaga, whose hatred of Buddhism was intense, had been especially friendly toward the Christians. Hideyoshi was much more sympathetic to Buddhism (he even restored various temples that had been razed by Nobunaga's armies), and remained a Buddhist throughout his life. But he did not object when two of his most trusted generals were converted to Christianity, and he even granted the foreigners a tract of land on which to build a church.

Soon after his successful campaign of 1587 in Kyushu, however, he suddenly ordered all missionaries to leave the country within twenty days. This decree was announced only a few hours after he had been drinking red wine with some missionaries. Why he made this sudden decision is unknown, but the extent of Christian penetration into Kyushu may have come as a shock to Hideyoshi, who was ever apprehensive about possible divisions in allegiance.

Later that year, he ordered the expulsion of all Christian missionaries from Nagasaki, which, thanks to foreign trade, had developed rapidly from an insignificant fishing port into an important city. This edict was carried out at the risk of destroying the city, for 70 per cent of the Japanese inhabitants were Christians, and most of the remainder traded with the Portuguese.

In response to the needs of Portuguese crews, who generally spent six months or so each year in Nagasaki waiting for favorable winds to take them home, shops had sprung up that made and sold Portuguese clothes, food, and

M. INOUI © TIME, INC.—FROM THE TIME-LIFE GREAT AGES OF MAN SERIES; OPPOSITE: CUIRASS, JITSUJO HAGA, TOKYO, SHOULDER GUARDS, USESUGI SHRINE, YAMAGATA PREFECTURE; COURTESY THE METROPOLITAN MUSEUM OF ART

A labyrinthine path leads toward the prime

onghold of Himeji—or White Heron—Castle. Begun in 1600, just after Hideyoshi's death, it was one of the last high-walled castles to be built in Japan.

Part of a Buddhist monastery destroyed by fire in 1470, the Sambo-in garden in Kyoto, above, was restored by Hideyoshi during the sixteenth century as a peaceful sanctuary. Its low-arched bridges, winding waterways, and meticulously pruned vegetation reflect the ruler's courtly tastes.

furniture. Some Portuguese goods introduced at that time are still known by Japanese approximations of the original Portuguese words, including *pan*, for bread (Portuguese *pão*), and *tabako* (Portuguese *tabaco*).

Portuguese influence extended to other areas as well. Three years after Hideyoshi's first anti-Christian decree, four Japanese youths who had been taken to Rome by Catholic priests returned to Japan with a group of Portuguese dignitaries, and in the spring of 1591 Hideyoshi received the party at his Mansion of Pleasures. The foreigners were magnificently attired for the occasion, and as they passed through the streets of Kyoto on their way to Hideyoshi's mansion, a great throng of people lined the roadway to catch a glimpse of them. A priest in the party, describing the triumphal parade in a letter sent back home, declared that for days afterward the only subject of conversation among the Japanese was the dress and appearance of the Europeans. Hideyoshi, he wrote, was so impressed by the clothes worn by his visitors that he thought the Japanese seemed to be beggars by comparison.

Allowing for some exaggeration, there is no doubt that the parade produced a stunning impression and led to a sudden vogue for Portuguese clothes. Young men of the upper classes wore European shirts, breeches, hats, and capes ordered from Nagasaki shops, and by the autumn of 1593 a priest wrote that anyone in the capital who did not own at least one item of Portuguese dress was looked down upon. Accessories such as amber beads and gold chains were also popular, and despite the anti-Christian decrees fashionable people frequently complemented their attire with rosaries and crucifixes. Okuni, the reputed founder of the Kabuki dances, often sported a crucifix when she performed, though she was nominally a Shinto priestess.

Hideyoshi himself was fond of Portuguese customs. One account describes how much he enjoyed eating beef (though Buddhist law prohibited it), and how he would dress for the occasion in a Portuguese costume. The craze for European things reflected Japanese curiosity about the people and customs of distant parts of the world. There was not much the Europeans of this time could teach the Japanese—the missionaries agreed that material conditions in Japan were far superior to those of Europe—but many items of their dress and food amused even the most sophisticated residents of the capital.

Despite this fascination with foreign goods and customs, religious persecution continued. In 1596, Hideyoshi heard a rumor that the proselytism of the Japanese by Portuguese Jesuits and Spanish Franciscans was designed as the first step in the conquest of Japan by the king of Spain. Alarmed, he ordered the arrest of twenty-six Spanish priests and converts in Kyoto. They were taken to Nagasaki in 1597, and there they were crucified—a grim warning that Hideyoshi would not tolerate disobedience of his orders.

Hideyoshi may have been determined not to allow foreign encroachments in Japan, but he was eager to expand Japanese territories abroad. For some years he had mulled over plans to conquer Korea and China. In 1586 he revealed his designs to a Portuguese missionary, explaining that victories overseas would assure that his name was remembered by posterity. He also asked the Portuguese to supply two large ships for the expedition, and in return, he promised to allow the Christianization of Korea and China. Orders for the attack were finally issued in 1592, and more than

158,000 Japanese soldiers were dispatched to Korea. At first the Japanese won easy victories, and Hideyoshi confidently predicted that China would fall by autumn. From his headquarters in Kyushu, he wrote that he expected to celebrate the Feast of Chrysanthemums that year in Peking.

Early in 1593, however, a large Chinese army defeated the overextended Japanese troops at Pyongyang. Japanese casualties were heavy, about a third of the entire force, and morale was so low that many soldiers deserted. Four years later, in 1597, Hideyoshi ordered a second invasion of Korea. Despite early Japanese victories, the war soon entered a period of stalemate. The following year the Japanese troops withdrew from Korea, leaving little behind except a lasting hatred of the Japanese.

Even as Hideyoshi's army was engaged in furious fighting in Korea, he sent letters to the Portuguese in Macao, the Spaniards in Manila, and the Chinese on Taiwan demanding tribute and threatening invasion if they refused. By these letters, Hideyoshi plainly revealed that his overseas ambitions were not confined to Korea and China. Japanese warlords of the time usually were satisfied to call one little corner of Japan their own, but Japan was too small for Hideyoshi, who once declared that after he had conquered China he would go on to India and Persia.

Hideyoshi's ambitions were only one aspect of his character. He was like no single figure in European history. He may remind us of Napoleon in his spectacular rise to power through his brilliance as a general, and his combination of sometimes barbaric cruelty with great sensitivity toward the arts recalls a number of Renaissance princes. Yet, for all his ferocity, he emerges from the pages of history as a warm and even appealing figure. In whatever he did, he was straightforward, often impulsive. His love of art, for example, was no mere affectation designed to conceal his lack of formal education, but an expression of his genuine attraction to the culture that had been denied him in his ear-

The Yu-in tea hut in Kyoto

THE WAY OF TEA

It is known in Japan as *cha-no-yu*, the tea ceremony. Peformed in a small, plain hut reached by a garden path of steppingstones, the ceremony is neither mysterious nor elaborate. The boiling of the water, the cleaning of the bowls, the preparation of the powdered green tea, the very conversation of the guests about the merits of the utensils, is fixed and formalized. The tea ceremony is a practical, not a symbolic, rite; yet for almost four centuries it has exerted a powerful influence on the soul of Japanese culture.

It was the gifted Sen no Rikyu, Hideyoshi's personal tea master, who first brought tea to all levels of Japanese society. In 1587 he erected eight hundred tea huts in Kyoto and held the Great Kitano Tea Meeting to which everyone, regardless of rank, was invited. And it was Rikyu who demonstrated that the art of serving and savoring tea could embody Japan's most cherished virtues—cleanliness, resourcefulness, and simplicity. Believing that beauty was to be found in the commonplace, he prescribed the rude hut as the proper setting for tea drinking and instituted the use of hand-molded ceramic bowls, called Raku ware, which are still being made today.

Because the mighty Hideyoshi was Rikyu's patron, Rikyu's "way of tea" became not only the nation's way but also a unique school of moral virtue —another mark, in Japanese eyes, of Hideyoshi's genius.

A tea bowl and bamboo whisk

lier years. His letters are filled with unmistakable affection for his mother, for his wife, and especially for his sons.

Hideyoshi was fifty-three when his first son, Tsurumatsu, was born in 1589. He doted on the boy, and the child's mother, Lady Yodo, became his favorite concubine. Unfortunately, Tsurumatsu died at the age of three. Hideyoshi must have been overjoyed, therefore, when Lady Yodo gave birth to another son in 1593. His letters are full of references to the boy, who was given the name Hiroi, or foundling, to allay the jealousy of the gods. When Hideyoshi was separated from Hiroi during his campaigns, he wrote long letters, telling how much he missed the child and how he yearned to take Hiroi in his arms and kiss him. And yet, Hideyoshi could be merciless. When his nephew allegedly harbored treacherous designs, he commanded him to commit suicide. His anger still unappeased, he ordered the nephew's many concubines to be summarily executed.

Considering his poor education and his long career as a soldier, Hideyoshi's interest in the peaceful arts was exceptional. Military men of the time often acquired some cultural refinement so as not to appear barbarous, but Hideyoshi's mania for culture far exceeded that of any other military man of his time. He studied poetry and encouraged poets, and supported the Noh drama and the decorative arts.

Above all, he loved the tea ceremony (see box, left). In 1587 he invited the entire city of Kyoto to the grounds of the Kitano Shrine for a giant tea party, the only requirement being that everyone must bring his own cup. Hideyoshi was also the patron of Sen no Rikyu, revered today as the greatest practitioner of the tea ceremony, and he studied the ritual assiduously, even though the understated manner of Rikyu's tea ceremony did not accord with Hideyoshi's flamboyant personality. Rikyu, who genuinely loved simplicity, must have felt very ill at ease when he was obliged to prepare tea in the glitter and splendor of Hideyoshi's golden teahouse.

TEXT CONTINUED ON PAGE 25

A dancer celebrates spring

KYOTO:
THE PLEASURES OF THE CAPITAL

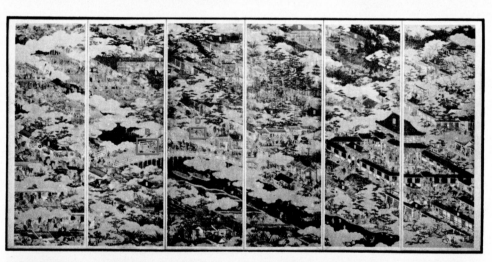

The two six-panel screens above, which extend some twenty-two feet when placed side by side, give a bird's-eye view of Kyoto. An unknown artist painted this panorama, called Activities in the Capital, *in about 1614, using clouds of gold leaf to separate the various vignettes of daily life. The details reproduced on the following pages correspond to the lettered boxes.*

Once Toyotomi Hideyoshi had made himself master of all Japan, the country was on its way to becoming a modern state. Bold, self-reliant, and imaginative, Hideyoshi ushered in an era of explosive energy and experiment. It was a brash, secular age, when artists cast off courtly decorum and feudal formalities and began, for the first time, to paint realistic scenes of daily life. It was also an age of commerce, when Europeans freely roamed the streets of Japan's cities and European customs were received with great enthusiasm.

It is the uninhibited exuberance of Hideyoshi's era—known as the Momoyama period in Japanese historiography—that the anonymous painter of the two screens on this page portrayed some sixteen years after Hideyoshi's death in 1598. When placed side by side and viewed from right to left (the upper screen first), they show Kyoto from Hideyoshi's Great Buddha Hall in the southeastern suburb of the city to the Nijo Castle of the mighty Tokugawa family. The distance between the two buildings may be a sly political comment on the part of the artist, for around 1614 Hideyoshi's followers were struggling bitterly with the Tokugawas for supreme power in Japan.

But politics is not the chief subject of the screens, any more than it was the chief concern of Kyoto at the time. The ancient city had long since become a mere titular capital, the home of an emperor who held no real power. But if Kyoto was no longer the seat of government, it could indisputably be called the capital of fashion, luxury, and pleasureful entertainments.

As the details on these pages show, Kyoto at the end of the Momoyama period was a city of shops selling everything from swords to hairpins. It was also a city of pastimes, boasting both a theatre district (above the bridge in the right-hand screen) and a thriving brothel district (directly below the bridge). Finally, it was a city of festivals and parades, such as the Gion festival with its procession of colorful silk brocade balloon-talismans, which were believed to ward off evil spirits.

But in every endeavor, Kyoto was a city bursting with vitality; Kyotoans, it is clear, endowed even the most humdrum activities with a furious energy. By portraying this energy so vigorously, the unknown screen painter has given posterity what is perhaps its most faithful testament to the spirit of Hideyoshi's era.

A. Carrying a huge brocade balloon, a warrior parades in the Gion festiv

B. *Cherry blossoms and fans aflutter, frenzied dancers cavort on a bridge. Picking blossoms and drinking were traditional rites of spring.*

C. *Opposite, dancers perform for courtiers and for the emperor, behind the screen.*

D. *Women take the roles in a Kabuki play, a new theatre form.*

E. *A woman agonizes over choosing hairpins; a samurai gets a haircut.*

F. *Mounted samurais raise havoc in a crowded street.*

G. *In the red-light district, prostitutes accost young samurais, while a reluctant passer-by seeks to escape notice by hiding behind his fan.*

Hideyoshi was equally infatuated with the Noh drama. Perfected toward the end of the fourteenth century, the Noh plays combine music and dance, and are usually brief evocations of the tragic lives of historical or legendary figures. Hideyoshi subsidized the theatre and his favorite actors, and also learned many of the roles. In Kyushu in 1592, awaiting a propitious moment to join his army in Korea, he studied ten difficult roles and, with no show of false modesty, wrote his consort that he had become skillful in all of them. Before long, he was confidently performing in public. When his son Hiroi was born, he not only arranged for three days of performances to celebrate the event but acted sixteen of the roles himself. On the second day he and Tokugawa Ieyasu appeared in a newly composed farce that was performed between two Noh tragedies. It is difficult to imagine the two most powerful military men in the country capering about a stage, but Hideyoshi had few inhibitions, and his enthusiasm may have affected the cautious and reserved Ieyasu.

Hideyoshi's fascination with the Noh theatre reached its height in 1594 when he performed in various plays at the imperial palace, including the most difficult works in the entire repertory. He also appeared in five new plays written by his official scribe to commemorate his own achievements. In one play he even took the leading role, acting out his triumph over the traitor Akechi Mitsuhide.

Hideyoshi was also an enthusiastic amateur poet. He wrote both the traditional tanka, a five-line poem of thirty-one syllables, and the more modern renga, or linked verse, composed of a series of alternating "links" in seventeen and fourteen syllables written by two or more poets in turn. In one letter he mentioned his difficulty in finding a suitable last line for a poem, a problem he took quite seriously. He was also eager to obtain the approval of professional poets, and since there was no dearth of sycophants at court, his poetry was extravagantly admired.

On one occasion Hideyoshi opened a linked-verse series with these lines: "As I tramp through red leaves/Deep in the mountains,/The fireflies are singing." The eminent statesman and poet Hosokawa Yusai at once added a link to Hideyoshi's lines, but someone in the gathering murmured that fireflies do not sing. Yusai insisted that there was textual evidence that fireflies did sing, and quoted an ancient poem that ended, "Apart from the fireflies no insect is singing." Hideyoshi's good humor, which had perceptibly faded when he heard the whispered criticism, was immediately restored. Some days later Yusai admitted that he had made up the "ancient poem" on the spot.

Hideyoshi's great interest in the visual arts is apparent in the innumerable paintings and sculptures that were

A blossom-and-leaf design forms the crest of Toyotomi Hideyoshi.

created at his command. Osaka Castle and the one known as Momoyama Castle, south of Kyoto at Fushimi, were imposing. The keep at Osaka was eight stories high and was surrounded by three moats. These castles were not only forts but also residences. Painted screens, the most typical art of the period, were used to brighten the rather bleak interiors. The most interesting of these vividly portray contemporary life, especially the sights inside and outside the capital. These scenes of Kyoto were originally painted as souvenirs for visitors, and later for the townspeople themselves, who also enjoyed seeing familiar locales and the day-to-day activities of tradesmen, priests, entertainers, and foreigners. The screens thus provide us with an incredibly detailed picture of what life was like in the capital during Hideyoshi's time. (One of the most magnificent of these screens, painted a few years after Hideyoshi's death, is *Activities in the Capital*, which appears in full on page 18 and in detail in the portfolio on pages 18 to 24.)

Hideyoshi was increasingly preoccupied at the end of his life with the question of who would succeed him. In 1595, 1596, and on his deathbed in 1598, he asked his major feudatories—including his former enemy and later ally, Ieyasu—to swear loyalty to his son, now called Hideyori. But he himself had displaced Oda Nobunaga's heir after promising to serve him faithfully, and he undoubtedly realized that these ambitious men were unlikely to keep their promises if they could seize power.

Two years after Hideyoshi's death, the opposing factions met at the Battle of Sekigahara, and the victor was Tokugawa Ieyasu. After the defeat of their allies, Lady Yodo and Hideyori remained in the castle at Osaka. Hideyori, who had none of his father's political ability, indulged himself in a life of eating, drinking, and lovemaking.

In 1614 Tokugawa Ieyasu, determined to dispose of even the insignificant threat represented by Hideyori, led an army of 200,000 men against Osaka Castle. The defenders fought bravely, and in the end won a truce. But fighting broke out again the following summer, and this time the attackers could not be held back. Hideyori and Lady Yodo were trapped in one of the towers, and Ieyasu refused to spare their lives. Hideyori committed suicide, and Lady Yodo had herself killed by a loyal retainer; they were followed in death by their entire retinue, men and women alike. And thus ended the line of Hideyoshi, which flourished briefly but brilliantly. Ieyasu took over the country Hideyoshi had unified, and founded a military government that was to last until 1867, when the shogunate would at last be replaced by imperial rule.

Donald Keene teaches at Columbia. His latest book is Landscapes and Portraits: Appreciations of Japanese Culture.

H. *Their trousers and hats mark the men in the foreground as Europeans.*

DEFEAT

By J. H. PLUMB

The last shots were fired in Saigon just two hundred years after the first shots were fired at Concord in April, 1775: the first victory and the first defeat, two centuries apart. There are strange resonances between the American Revolution and Vietnam. Both were essentially guerrilla wars in which victory came to the weak, for the military might and financial resources of Britain in the eighteenth century were as formidable as those of America in the twentieth. Neither America nor North Vietnam could have succeeded without the aid of great powers, France and Spain on the one hand, China and Russia on the other. Both times the losers, Britain and America, had sharp divisions within their own peoples, creating a partial paralysis of will.

The resonances are, indeed, deep and sonorous. But there is at least one discordance. It is hard to imagine American museums mounting exhibition after exhibition to recall and celebrate the defeat in Vietnam, as British museums are doing this year, busily recalling the humiliations of 1775–83. Even though the British—never defeated in war since—have come to accept the loss of America with considerable sang-froid, this was far from true at the time. Defeats are always traumatic; they give rise to noisy lamentations and more often than not have surprising results. Yet all nations experience defeat. Trauma is as much a part of national life as it is of personal life.

Up to now America has escaped many of the traumas that have been so constant a factor in the histories of most

Above, the British surrender at Yorktown in October of 1781; below, American evacuees leave Saigon by helicopter in April, 1975.

other nations: famine, revolution, occupation by foreign armies, devastation, rapine and pillage, bombing and slaughter, repeated civil war. For the last one hundred and fifty years there has not been a generation of Frenchmen that has not endured one or another of these disasters, but the French people today are as ardent in their pursuit of happiness as they ever were. And yet, as

recently as 1940 France experienced its most terrible defeat since the late Middle Ages. That West Germany and Japan soared like phoenixes from their ashes has, for decades now, been a wonder to the world. Perhaps even more remarkable is the capacity with which West Germany, far from savage toward individual Nazis, disengaged itself from its past and created a workable, federal democracy whose political strength has so far proved as efficacious as its economy. Germany's defeat was more total, more traumatic, than military defeats usually are, and, as sometimes happens with personal traumas, there is in Germany a discontinuity of memory, an inability to recall the hours of suffering.

It is more customary for defeats to give rise to an orgy of national soul-searching: publicists harp on moral weakness, the collapse of will, even the anger of Providence at a profligate way of life. In 1776 the British writer Dr. Richard Price had not the slightest doubt whose side Providence would favor. "What are we doing?" he asked his countrymen, and answered quickly:

Shocking thought—we are running wild after pleasure and forgetting everything serious and decent in Masquerades—we are gambling in gaming houses; trafficking in boroughs; perjuring ourselves at elections; and selling ourselves for places—which side is Providence likely to favour?

America, of course, for the simple reason that "from one end of North America to the other they are praying and fasting." Nor was Dr. Price alone in thinking that England would not catch the eye of the God of Victories again until the members of the aristocracy finally reformed their morals and the workingmen stopped drinking and gambling and took to prayer.

Dr. Price and his supporters were, of course, heirs to an ancient tradition that stretches back to Saint Augustine, if not beyond. Saint Augustine had little difficulty in pinpointing the causes for the defeat of the Roman Imperial legions at the hands of the barbarians: the licentiousness of the ruling classes, a population besotted with worldly pleasures, the lack of any sense of personal austerity or dedication to a higher destiny. The pursuit of happiness, if rooted in the sensual delights of this world, could only end in defeat, a necessary punishment of a just God. It is not surprising, then, that as soon as General de Gaulle came to power in 1945, he closed the licensed brothels of France.

Indeed, wherever one looks in history, the attitude of Dr. Price, of Saint Augustine, of General de Gaulle, seems to acquire substance. The austere armies of Islam sweeping away the decadent relics of the ancient world, Cromwell's Ironsides drunk on prayer, the exemplary puritanism of Mao's Long Marchers—these are surely proof enough that sensual delights, and abstinence from them, are reflected in the results of war. It would seem that "decadence" and "defeat" may be closely linked, or at least be first cousins.

Sometimes the argument is given a subtler twist. The direct link is not stressed, but the question is asked: How can military victory impose a way of life upon a people that does not want it? Whatever may happen at the military level, there will be a moral defeat unless people desire, or at least admire and respect, the way of life represented by the military forces. How can the peasants of the Mekong Delta admire or desire the gross self-indulgence of American life—from the massage parlors of New York to the Watergate scandals of Washington? At the moral level, could Americanized Saigon ever compete with communized Hanoi: one

dedicated to personal profit and immoral exploitation; the other to sacrifice, education, and social achievement?

It is an attractive argument, this, which associates moral commitment and personal austerity with victory. Certainly the morally austere do have victories, but so, in the light of the past, do the sensual and the profane, so do societies and elites rioting in sexual indulgence and financial corruption. After all, when young General Bonaparte swept through northern Italy, winning battle after battle, he did not leave behind a Paris or a government, or a society for that matter, notable for its austerity. The Directoire's sexual license was matched only by its financial corruption, and when the Directoire was swept away by Napoleon, morals did not change. Neither the emperor, his family, nor his marshals were averse to the accumulation of money by almost any means or to the blatant indulgence of their sexual appetites. Yet no nation has had a greater string of victories, and it would be hard to conclude that the debacle in 1812 was caused by the decadent state of French society.

Nor do the great wars of this century bear out the thesis that moral decadence leads to defeat. Whatever may be said of Hitler personally, he imposed a strict morality on the citizens of the Third Reich. Stalin's Russia was not marked by a reckless indulgence of sexual appetites, for divorce and abortion, let alone prostitution and sexual deviance, had been made difficult and socially reprehensible; but the same cannot be said of Russia's Western allies. British and American societies in the twenties and thirties tolerated a far greater degree of sexual license than previous generations had. Nor were these societies free from political corruption and financial skullduggery. Yet the Allies won, and the Germans lost. Such an argument, therefore, leads us nowhere. Nor would Hitler's belief that defeat springs from a corruption of the will to victory take us much further. After all, the answer to that argument is contained in the ruins

of the Berlin bunker, or, even more grimly, in the ashes of Hiroshima.

There is no easy explanation of defeats. Social division, lack of commitment, weak armies, wrong decisions, even bad luck and a host of other circumstances may lead to the defeat of a nation. The real dangers of defeat do not always lie in the defeat itself, but in the way it may be exploited. There is always a hunger in any society to discover a simple answer or to punish a scapegoat. After all, defeat breeds guilt, breeds myths, breeds also a sense of inferiority. Defeat can rarely, if ever, be accepted as a material fact springing from material causes; it is easier to accept as a punishment by God, as a consequence of moral failure, or a weakness of the will. Such imponderables have always attracted social activists: men and women confident in their interpretation of God's will; others absolutely certain of their moral judgments as to what should or should not be permitted in a society that wishes to impose itself on the world; still others eager to strengthen the nation's backbone by taking it in the grip of their own iron authority.

Defeats, like traumas, are not easily assimilated or forgotten; their scars last. One of the most powerful responses to the defeat in Vietnam may be the argument, increasingly well-publicized, that the American society not only lacks appeal but, with its emphasis on permissiveness and consumer wealth, is completely counterproductive: it makes people hate, not love. This much may be granted: very probably, it is not a way of life that can make much sense to a poverty-stricken peasant in the Mekong Delta. While admitting this, it is well to remember the Berlin Wall, which was built to prevent thousands of East Germans from fleeing to enjoy the delights of American-style civilization. Thus, what may be meaningless in one context may be compelling in another. An image must always fail if its message is meaningless to those at whom it is directed. Lack of political and social intelligence is far more responsible for defeat than moral turpitude.

27

OF
NOMADS
AND
KNIGHTS

This ancient plaque from Siberia may link the heritage of the
Russian steppes to King Arthur and the chivalric tradition

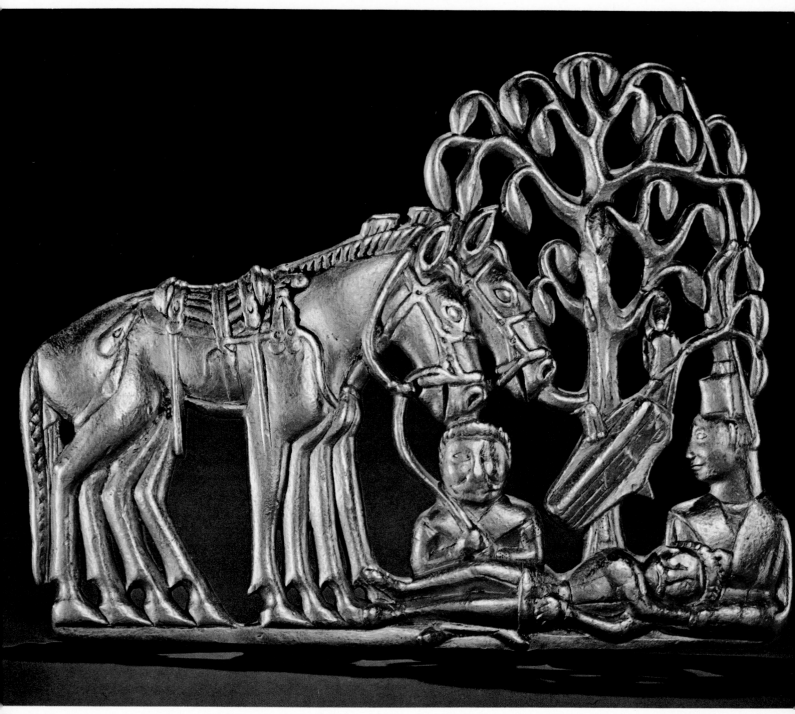

Gold plaque, one of a pair made around 300 B.C., possibly for use as a scabbard mount

An idyllic moment is frozen in gold. A warrior sleeps, his head in his lady's lap, his bow-and-arrow case hung in the branches of a sheltering tree. A second man, perhaps a groom, waits patiently, holding the reins of the horses. Stillness pervades the scene. We are witnessing a pause in some headlong flight, perhaps, or the sleep of a warrior before battle.

The gold plaque on the opposite page and its mirror-image mate were made in Siberia about 300 B.C. Part of a gold hoard from an ancient burial mound, they were discovered early in the eighteenth century, probably by tomb robbers. Some time before 1726, identified merely as "golden idols from the Siberian hills," they made their way into the hands of Peter the Great. Today the plaques are part of the famous collection of Scythian gold at the Hermitage in Leningrad, a treasure that was recently lent by the Soviet government for exhibit at the Metropolitan Museum of Art in New York and at the Los Angeles County Museum.

No one is certain what the plaque represents, or even what it was made for. Does the scene come from some otherwise unknown Central Asian epic? Was the plaque part of a belt buckle, or part of a harness? Was it a piece of jewelry? Dr. Helmut Nickel, curator of arms and armor at the Metropolitan Museum, who has closely studied the works of the Scythian exhibition, has suggested an answer. The plaque and its mate, he thinks, were intended as attachments for sword scabbards, and the sleeping warrior may link an epic tradition of the early Siberian nomads to the much later phenomenon of chivalry in medieval Europe.

Little is known about the ancient Siberians. Much of what we can conjecture about them comes from our knowledge of the Scythians. They, and many other tribes of mounted warriors, roamed the steppes in the first millennium B.C. It seems likely that the Scythians originally came from Siberia. By the seventh century B.C. they had moved as far west as the area south of the Caucasus and were known to the As-

syrians. In the fifth century B.C., Herodotus wrote this richly lurid account of the Scythians:

Having neither cities nor forts, and carrying their dwellings with them wherever they go; accustomed, moreover, one and all of them, to shoot from horseback; and living not by husbandry but on their cattle, their wagons the only houses that they possess: how can they fail of being unconquerable, and unassailable even?

According to Herodotus, the Scythians made short work of those they killed in battle. Flaying them, they used their skin to make coverings for quivers. The scalps were stitched together to make cloaks. As Herodotus explains: "The

A Siberian cavalier, circa 500 B.C.

skin of a man is thick and glossy, and would in whiteness surpass almost all other hides."

Herodotus also tells us that the Scythians held gold to be sacred, and made sacrifices to it. When a Scythian ruler died he was buried in a great mound, accompanied by a concubine, servants, horses, and gold objects. A year later, according to custom, fifty young men and fifty horses were killed and arranged around the mound "as a final token of the late king's power over his people."

Among the objects that have been found in such burial mounds are scabbards with P-shaped attachment mounts, used to sheathe the short swords that Scythian horsemen carried into battle. A pair of such gold plaques,

fastened together back to back on the leather flap of a scabbard, could have attached a single sword to a warrior's belt. Or, if they were used separately, they could have attached two swords to his belt, one on each hip.

Archaeologists, tracing the P-shaped scabbard mounts hundreds of years beyond the time of Herodotus to the great barbarian migrations of the fourth century A.D., have found them all the way from Central Europe to China, wherever, in fact, steppe nomads roamed. Among the Huns, for example, the most widely known of the tribes to pour out of Asia in the fourth century, it was the custom to wear a pair of swords, one on each hip. Although the Huns were lost to history shortly after the death of their famous king Attila in A.D. 453, they lived on in legend—and reappeared, Dr. Nickel suggests, in a medieval epic of the tenth century known as *Waltharius*. This poem, the oldest preserved portion of the Nibelungen cycle, is surely connected with the scene of idyllic ease on the Siberian plaque.

In *Waltharius* the hero of that name, who is a Visigothic prince of Aquitaine, is held hostage by Attila the Hun, along with his betrothed, the princess Hildegund. Waltharius has armed himself in Hunnish fashion with two swords, and together he and the princess flee their captors. Reaching the safety of the Vosges forest, Waltharius stops to rest. He asks Hildegund to wake him if she sees the dust of approaching horsemen; he puts his head in her lap, and sleeps.

Seeing horsemen riding toward them, Hildegund wakes Waltharius. The horsemen, as it turns out, are not Huns but a party of marauding Franks. Waltharius takes them on and in a fearful battle kills twelve of the raiders. At length, his first sword shatters and his Frankish assailant cuts off Waltharius's hand. Imperturbable, Waltharius hooks his shield over the stump of his arm, unsheathes his second sword, and fights to a draw. Hildegund binds up the wounds of both men and they lightheartedly make peace.

Clearly recognizable in this tale is

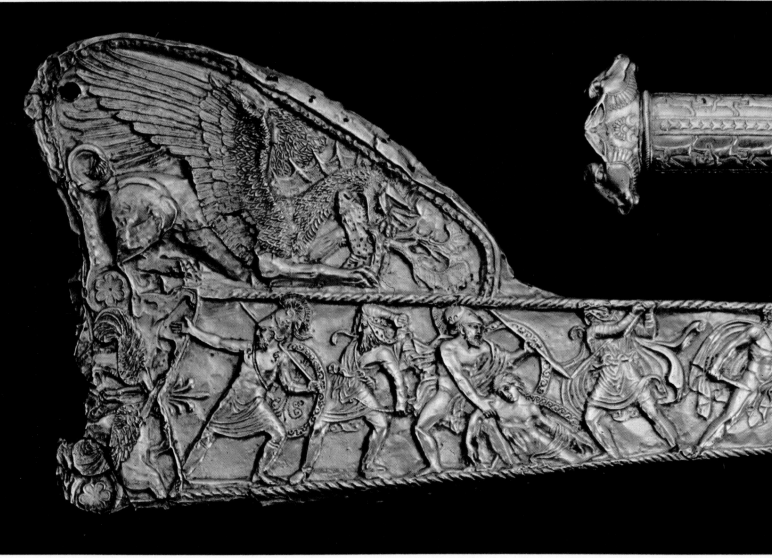

A Scythian lord wore this splendid gold scabbard of Greek workmanship, which hung from his belt by a thong, as in the plaque below left. A grif

the distinctive scene on the Siberian plaque, as well as the nomadic custom of wearing two swords. That same custom and some version of the same legend could surely have existed among the Siberian nomads. The story might well have made its way west as part of an oral tradition, later to be written down by some unknown scribe in medieval Europe.

The plaque may have other connections as well. Dr. Nickel believes that it may even be linked to the Arthurian legends, for the warrior with two swords, lying with his head in his lady's lap beneath a tree, appears in the stories of Parsifal and other knights of the Holy Grail. The

Scythian warrior with sword and scabbard

clue here lies with the Sarmatians, another tribe of steppe nomads like the Scythians. By the second and first centuries B.C. the Sarmatians had conquered much of Scythian territory and had moved as far west as the Danube. In A.D. 175, on the banks of the Danube, the redoubtable Sarmatian armored cavalry met the armies of Marcus Aurelius, and were soundly defeated by superior Roman generalship. According to the terms of peace, fifty-five hundred Sarmatian cavalrymen were taken away to serve in the Roman army in Britain and fought the Picts on the northern border. They never returned, and their descendants appear in military records as late as

the fifth century A.D. According to Dr. Nickel, they may well have made their mark upon the culture of Britain, for certain elements of Sarmatian custom and lore bear an odd resemblance to the Arthurian stories.

First of all, the Sarmatians served in Britain under a Roman commander named Lucius Artorius Castus. "Possibly," Nickel writes, "they turned his name, Artorius, into a title—the way

Tombstone of a Sarmatian chief, found in northwestern England

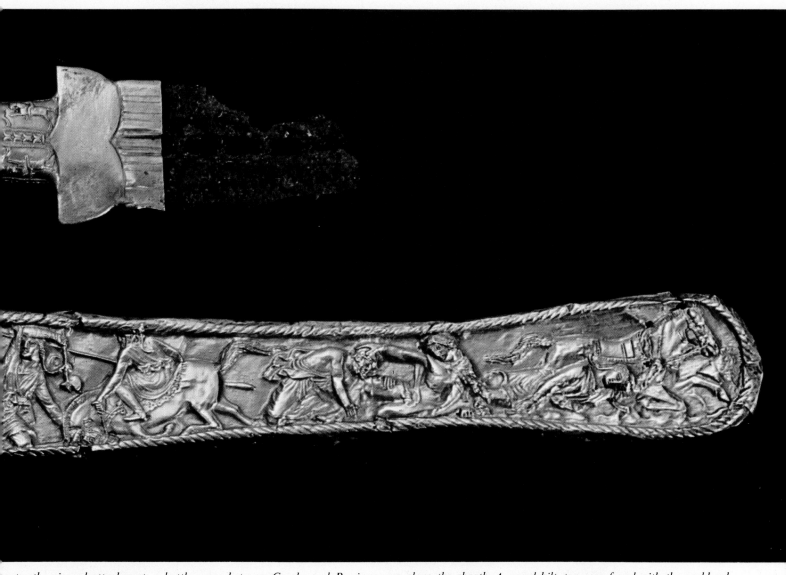

...rates the pierced attachment; a battle scene between Greeks and Persians runs along the sheath. A sword hilt, top, was found with the scabbard.

Caesar became Kaiser and Tsar. During the fifth century, when the 'historical' Arthur is supposed to have lived, this title might have been used by a great British chieftain." If so, at least we know how the hero came by his name. Secondly, the battle standard of the Sarmatians was a dragon, made like a windsock, with a red fabric body and a metal head. The legendary Arthur, son of Uther Pendragon, carries a dragon on his battle standard, too. Furthermore, the name of Arthur's sword, Excalibur, is derived from the Latin *chalybs*—for steel—via a Greek word derived from *Kalybes*, the name of a tribe of Sarmatian smiths in the Caucasus. Finally, the Sarmatian tribal god was worshiped in the form of a sword thrust upright into a stone platform. King

Arthur, of course, proves his royal identity by pulling Excalibur from a stone.

Here, then, is a remarkable set of clues connecting two of the great medieval heroes, Waltharius and King Arthur, with the nomads of the Eurasian

In this thirteenth-century miniature, Arthur at top pulls the sword from the stone; below, he is crowned king.

steppes. Perhaps even the concept of chivalry, so long thought to be rooted in the Middle Ages, reaches back as far as the first millennium B.C. For the rude barbarian and the medieval knight have at least this much in common: both were mounted warriors proud of their splendid steeds, and both regarded themselves as vastly superior to the man on foot or the tiller of the soil.

The Siberian nomads, the Scythians, the Huns, the Sarmatians—all vanished long ago, leaving virtually nothing of themselves except a few horse trappings, personal ornaments, and a bad reputation. But these "barbarians" had a culture (as no one who looks at the Scythian gold can doubt), and our own civilization may be more deeply indebted to it than we know.

31

THE WILD BOY OF AVEYRON

What is the nature of man?
For the answer to this central question,
Enlightenment philosophers
looked to a deaf-mute child found
running wild in a forest

By HARLAN LANE

One day in 1797, in the fifth year of the new French Republic, peasants in the region of Lacaune, in south-central France, spied a naked boy fleeing through the woods. Their curiosity aroused, they lay in wait on the following days and finally saw him searching for acorns and roots. In 1798 he was sighted again by woodsmen and, despite violent resistance, taken to the village of Lacaune, where his arrival created a sensation. He was put on display several times in the public square, but the crowd's curiosity was quickly satisfied by the sight of the filthy mute urchin, and under relaxed surveillance he was able to escape into the forest.

Over the next fifteen months the wild boy was seen from time to time in the fields on the edge of the forest, digging up potatoes and turnips, which he ate on the spot or occasionally carried off. Several lairs were found and attributed to him, including one with a bed of leaves and moss. Then, on July 25, 1799, three hunters spotted him in the same woods, gave chase, and succeeded in dislodging him from a tree. Securely tied, he was led back to Lacaune and entrusted to the care of an old widow. This devoted guardian dressed him in a gown to hide his nakedness and offered him various foods, including raw and cooked meat, which he refused. He did accept acorns, chestnuts, walnuts, and potatoes, always sniffing them before putting them in his mouth. When not eating or sleeping, he prowled from door to door and window to window seeking to escape. After eight days, he succeeded.

This time the wild boy did not return to the forest. Climbing the nearby mountains, he gained the broad plateau between Lacaune and Roquecézière, in the department of Aveyron. Through the autumn, and into a particularly cold winter, he wandered over this elevated and sparsely populated region, occasionally entering farmhouses where he was fed. When given potatoes, he threw them into the coals of the hearth, retrieving and eating them a few minutes later. During the day, he was seen swimming and drinking in streams, climbing trees, running at great speed on all fours, and digging for roots and bulbs in the fields. When the wind blew from the Midi, he would turn toward the sky and render deep cries and great bursts of laughter. Finally, working his way down the mountain along the course of the Lavergne and Vernoubre rivers, he arrived on the outskirts of the village of Saint-Sernin. Encouraged perhaps by the treatment he had received from the farmers on the plateau, and urged on perhaps by hunger, he approached the workshop of a dyer named Vidal. At seven o'clock on the morning of January 8, 1800, the boy slipped across the threshold into a new life, and into a new era in the education of man.

Word of the extraordinary wild boy spread rapidly, not only in the provinces but in Paris where several newspapers and most of the intelligentsia took up the theme of the *"enfant sauvage de l'Aveyron."* Never was a name more unsuitable, or so much responsible for later confusion. In the first place, the *"enfant"* was already an adolescent, some twelve to fifteen years of age. In the second place, he was not from Aveyron. But most important is the label *"sauvage,"* which could refer equally to wild animals, primitive people such as the Tahitians, and original man such as Rousseau's noble savage. The *enfant sauvage* was later to be identified with each of these in turn and was, of course, none of them. A sketch of his appearance and a presentiment of the tangled philosophical issues surrounding him may be had from a newspaper article published two days after his arrival in Paris, where he was soon enrolled, on orders of the minister of the interior, in a school for deaf mutes:

As yet we know very little about the child, who will now be the object of observations by true philosophers and who will surely be visited promptly by those who have long desired to raise a child cut off from all of society and all intellectual communication, a child to whom no one had ever spoken and who would be scrutinized down to the slightest movements he might make to express his first sensations, his first ideas, his first thoughts—if indeed one can think without fixed and conventional signs. . . .

The boy has a nice enough body, reasonably well developed, but he is completely bundled up like a three-year-old child, although he appears to be twelve, since he has never been willing to tolerate any other garment. This sort of body sheath is encircled by a broad belt; he does not wear shoes and stockings and is unwilling to wear any. He normally sits on the ground and lies there as well to sleep, and it was only to oblige his old guardian, whom he appears to love very much, that he sometimes sits on a chair or consents to spend the night in a bed. . . . He occasionally seems touched by the care he is tendered, and he offers his hand of his own accord to those who express any interest in him. But nothing can console him for the loss of his freedom and his way of life, and he seems as desirous as ever of escaping.

Over the next five years he would help answer the central question of the Enlightenment: What is the nature of man? Three issues were epitomized by the names of Linnaeus, Descartes, and Rousseau. In his *Systema naturae*, published in 1735, Linnaeus had scandalously placed man and the primates within the same order. Man was at the top of the list, to be sure, in recognition of his privileged position in the animal kingdom, but this did little to appease those Enlightenment philosophers who saw a "slippery slope" in the continuity of the species and in any affirmation of the animal nature of man. Their unease was amply justified, since man, in the latter half of the eighteenth century, found himself squarely in the company of wild animals, primitive people, and wild children.

All this served to sharpen such questions as: What makes us men? What are our relationships with the rest of creation? What are the criteria for membership in the human species? Is the difference between man and animal one of kind or one of degree? What can be learned from these beings that are at the same time like and unlike man? If men —not only scholars but laymen—found this humanoid diversity disquieting, they also felt that it might hold the key to an understanding of their own humanity.

The search for terms of comparison led out of society and into near and distant wilds. Numerous expeditions returned with samples of alien flora and fauna, including a parade of orangutans, gorillas, and chimps, as well as Pygmies and Hottentots, all of whom were subjected to detailed naturalistic and anatomical observation. Orangutans (whose name comes from the Malaysian and means wild man) were especially prized. Wild children were studied with equal zeal. Linnaeus, for example, reviews nine scantily documented cases. Rousseau cites five examples: the wolf child of Hesse (discovered in 1344); the wolf child of Lithuania (1694); two children found in the Pyrenees (1719); and the wild child Peter of Hanover (1794). The woods rendered up another child who received wide discussion and study in Paris before the wild boy of Aveyron arrived, the girl of Sogny, Mlle. Le Blanc. The growing body of comparative data and analysis tended to undermine the standing of the traditional criteria for manhood: human appearance, vertical station, and speech. The behavior of wild children was critical in the controversy.

They were equally relevant to a second major controversy of the times, associated with the name of Descartes: the existence of innate ideas. Some hoped to learn from wild children the secret of what man was like before language, what his ideas were like before they were filtered and shaped by convention. Did man, for instance, have an innate idea of God? Such inquiries were frustrated, of course, by the wild children's mutism. The girl from Sogny, captured in 1731 after spending some years in the wild with a companion, did later acquire language. The validity of the available descriptions is doubtful, but in any event, when asked, she revealed that she did not initially have an idea of the Supreme Being. (She rapidly acquired one, however, no doubt abetted by the

33

nuns who were responsible for her care.)

The third great controversy of the Enlightenment that focused attention on wild children concerned man in society. According to one view, man was nothing without society. The opposing view, which Rousseau's name evokes, emphasizes the many ills that man contracts in the process of socialization. A wild child testifies to the extraordinary physical resistance of natural man, able to live naked and without protection in the most rigorous climate, enjoying robust health, free of the many vices of society. Most philosophers rejected the concept of man in the state of nature, but for Rousseau and Kant there had been an era in which "the state of culture necessary to family life did not exist, where man lived in the wilds and children did not emit the birth cry for fear of detection by predators." Was the wild child an atavism of the noble savages?

Rousseau had an idea, however poorly documented, of what wild children were like, and it is doubtful that he saw in their traits a throwback to the nature of man before it was corrupted or masked by artificial education. In the perspective of man as a social animal, the wild child does not pose a problem. However, if society is not the natural end of man but the fruit of an accident, then why should social isolation have such disastrous consequences? Thus most observers expected to find, with the wild boy of Aveyron, more evidence that man in the state of nature would be an ignoble savage; that, in any event, this state could never have existed because man is so patently disenfranchised of his humanity when outside society. If man is perfectible, it is only as a social animal.

All efforts to obtain definite information about the origins of the wild boy were unsuccessful. The leading psychiatrists of the time examined him and concluded he was not a savage at all, but a retarded child abandoned by heartless parents. On the other hand, a police report from Aveyron for May 16, 1799 —two years before the wild boy was

captured—describes a ten-year-old nude boy who had "from all appearances hidden in the woods for five years surviving on roots and wild fruit." The boy explained that he had been obliged to flee home as a child "at a time when everyone was being killed." If it was the same boy who appeared in Saint-Sernin two years later, it seems clear that the wild boy was not abandoned because he was retarded. Under any circumstances, it is hard to see how a severely retarded five-year-old could survive alone in the forests.

Whatever the case, he was eventually transferred to the Institute for Deaf Mutes and given into the care of a twenty-six-year-old doctor named Jean Marc Gaspard Itard. Itard's association with the Institute had begun early in 1800 when a student had been hurt. The Abbé Sicard, the director, sent urgently for the nearest doctor, the young surgeon arrived, and a friendship sprang up between the novice physician and the renowned linguist-educator. Sicard created the post of resident physician at the Institute and appointed Itard to the position on December 31, 1800. As the new year arrived, the young physician took up the training of the *enfant sauvage* from Aveyron.

Itard was ready to attempt the boy's education, even when others were convinced of its futility, because he had already formed opinions on the metaphysical questions of the Enlightenment. In particular, he held the sensualist philosophy expounded by the philosopher Etienne Bonnot de Condillac in his *Essay on the Origin of Human Knowledge.*

The *enfant sauvage*, in this system, was not necessarily defective; he merely needed language if he was to perform the higher mental processes. Cut off from society, from social intercourse, and from language, having lived in the wilds for nearly half his life, the savage was nothing other than what he had to be. Itard reasoned:

If it were proposed to solve the following problem of metaphysics, to "determine what would be the degree of intelligence and the nature of the ideas of an adolescent who, deprived since infancy of any education, had lived entirely separated from individuals of his own species," then unless I am greatly mistaken, the solution of the problem would be as follows: There should first be assigned to that individual nothing but an intelligence relative to the small number of his needs and one deprived by isolation of all the simple and complex ideas we receive from education, which combine in our mind in so many ways solely by means of our knowledge of signs. Well, the mental status of this adolescent would be that of the wild boy of Aveyron.

Itard set down five principal aims for his training program:

1st Aim. To interest [the wild boy] in social life by rendering it more pleasant for him than the one he was leading, and above all more like the life he had just left.

2nd Aim. To awaken his nervous sensibility by the most energetic stimulation, and occasionally by intense emotion.

3rd Aim. To extend the range of his ideas by giving him new needs and by increasing his social contacts.

4th Aim. To lead him to the use of speech by subjecting him to the necessity of imitation.

5th Aim. To make him exercise the simplest mental operations, first concerning objects of his physical needs and later the objects of instruction.

In pursuit of the first goal, Itard took the boy into his home, a few blocks from the Institute, and charged the housekeeper with his daily care. The housekeeper, Madame Guérin, treated him kindly and gave in to his tastes and inclinations "with all the patience of a mother and the intelligence of an enlightened teacher." The boy was put to bed at dusk, provided with his favorite foods, allowed to be indolent, and taken on frequent walks in the adjacent Luxembourg Gardens.

Gradually Itard reduced the time devoted to bed, excursions, and food, and, with an eye to his second goal, took up the instruction proper. He turned first to the senses, the portals of the mind. Condillac provided that the first operation of the mind is perception and the second, attention, from which all other mental processes arise. Thus, confronted with the boy's failure to respond to all manner of stimuli, Itard undertook to "prepare the mind for attention by preparing the sense to receive keener impressions." In order to awaken the wild boy's "nervous sensibility by the most energetic stimulation," Itard administered hot baths, lasting two to three hours daily; he also clothed, bedded, and housed the boy warmly, and gave him massages of the spine and lumbar regions (although he soon discontinued the latter when he discovered they were sexually arousing for the boy).

Three months of this treatment, which also included provoking joy and anger on occasion, resulted in "a general excitement of all the senses." The boy would test the bath water with his finger and refuse to get in if it was cool. He removed potatoes from the fire with a spoon and squeezed them to judge how well cooked they were. He dropped burning paper before the flame could reach his fingers. He liked to stroke velvet. Though his sight and hearing were unchanged, his sense of smell had improved. "The least irritation of this organ provoked sneezing, and I judged by the fright that seized him the first time this happened that this was a new experience for him. He immediately ran away and threw himself on his bed. The refinement of the sense of taste was even more marked." The boy accepted a wider range of foods and kept them fastidiously clean. Itard capitalized on this newly acquired sensitivity to encourage some new habits by means of avoidance conditioning, as it is now called. The boy was left exposed to the cold each morning within reach of his clothes, and he soon learned to put them on. For much the same reason, he would get up in the night to urinate rather than sleep in a cold, wet bed.

In adopting his third aim, to lead the boy to acquire new needs, Itard slowly came to realize that the way to attach value to an object or event is to associate it with a primary reinforcer, such as food. This he did with notable success in a game of "shells."

I placed before him without any symmetrical order, and upside down, several little silver cups, under one of which I put a chestnut. Quite sure of having attracted his attention, I raised them one after the other except the one that covered the nut. After having thus shown him that they contained nothing, and having replaced them in the same order, I invited him by signs to seek in his turn for the chestnut. The first cup that he chose was precisely the one under which I had hidden the little reward for his attentiveness. Thus far, he showed only a feeble effort of memory. But I made the game imperceptibly more

Dr. Itard, the long-suffering physician who tried for five years to train the wild boy

complicated. Thus after having hidden another chestnut by the same procedure I changed the order of all the cups, slowly, however, so that in this general inversion he was able, although with difficulty, to follow with his eyes and with his attention the one that hid the precious object. I did more; I placed nuts under two or three of the cups and his attention, although divided between these three objects, followed them nevertheless in their respective changes, and directed his first searches toward them.

It is hard to believe we are reading about the same boy whose gaze could not fixate, and who had a short attention span and no memory.

In order to lead the boy to speak by imitating what he heard—Itard's fourth aim—the teacher realized that his pupil would first have to detect and distinguish speech sounds. Whereas originally the boy responded only to sounds associated with food and release from confinement, he increasingly reacted to voices. This growing sensitivity finally earned the wild boy a name:

One day when he was in the kitchen occupied with cooking potatoes two people had a sharp dispute behind him, without his appearing to pay the least attention. A third arrived to join the discussion who began all his replies with these words, "Oh, that's different!" I noticed that every time that this person let his favorite "Oh!" escape, the Savage of Aveyron quickly turned his head. That evening when he went to bed I experimented with this sound and obtained almost the same results. I went over all the other simple sounds known as vowels, but without any success. The preference for "o" obliged me to give him a name which ended with this vowel. I chose Victor. This name stuck, and when it is spoken aloud he rarely fails to turn his head or to come running.

Despite these gradual improvements in hearing, however, the boy remained mute, and Itard was ultimately to abandon him to incurable mutism.

Itard now undertook his fifth and final aim in the initial period of instruction, training at least some of the essential higher mental operations. At one point, his rapid progress in leading Victor to ever finer discriminations of shape and color emboldened the teacher to go too far too fast:

My persistence lasted only for a few days and was finally overcome by his independence of character. His fits of anger became more frequent, more violent. . . . He ran off and bit the sheets, the blankets, and the mantelpiece, scattered the andirons, ashes, and blazing embers, and ended by falling into convulsions which, like those of epilepsy, involved a complete suspension of sensory function. I was obliged to yield when things reached this frightful pitch; but my acquiescence only increased the evil. The paroxysms became more frequent, and apt to be renewed at the slightest opposition, often without any clear cause.

The teacher realized that by acquiescing in the disruptive behavior, he was strengthening it. He decided to try a

"He Has a Very Pleasant Laugh"

In 1800 two naturalists, Pierre-Joseph Bonnaterre and J. J. Virey, published firsthand accounts of the wild boy of Aveyron's appearance and behavior. In the excerpts below, Virey's observations are in italics.

He is 136 centimeters [4½ feet] tall: he appears to be twelve or thirteen years old. He has a light complexion; a round face; he has dark deep-set eyes; long eyelashes; brown hair; a long, somewhat pointed nose, an average mouth; a round chin; an agreeable visage and a pleasant smile. His tongue moves freely and shows no deformity. His whole body is covered with scars, of which the greater part seem to have been produced by burns.

When he raises his head, there will be seen, at the upper extremity of the trachea and on the middle of the glottis, a horizontal scar of some 41 millimeters [about an inch and two-thirds] in length, which seems to be the scar of a wound made with a cutting instrument. Did some barbaric hand, having led the child into the wilds, strike him with a death-dealing blade to render his loss more certain and more complete?

If these numerous scars are not an irrefutable proof of the bad treatment he suffered and of the attempts made to destroy him, they prove at least that he had no garments while he lived in the forest; and that his body must have been that much more vulnerable to scarring since he was not at all protected against the attack of animals, the mordant points of thorns, the cutting edges of rocks, and the density of the undergrowth.

However serious his wounds were, there appears to be no significant external deformity; and if his right knee is turned somewhat inward toward the other and the leg outward, which gives him a vacillating and unstable gait, this should probably be attributed to rheumatism caused by the humidity and the severe cold he has experienced.

When walking, or rather when trotting more or less rapidly—for he does not normally walk steadily—he rocks from one side to the other, which greatly facilitates his progress, as it does with runners. He is never winded. When he runs, he does not seem to pay much attention to his path; he does not falter, however, and he avoids obstacles without collision. He prefers shortcuts to the beaten track. If he sees some woods, he makes every effort to escape into them, uttering cries of joy, desire, and distress.

When he is seated, and even when he eats, he lets out a guttural sound, a dull murmur; and he rocks his body in an oscillatory movement from right to left or from front to back, holding his head high, his chin forward, his eyes fixed, and his lips closed. In this position, he occasionally undergoes spasms, some kind of convulsive fits, which seems to indicate that the nervous system is affected.

Otherwise, his organs seem normal and his senses good. Certain persons had believed that he was deaf, since he neither turns nor responds to shouts and questions addressed to him; but on reflection we can conceive that his ears, although normally formed, are much less useful to him because of his defective speech mechanism.

Taste being an interior sense of smell and consequently more related to the appetite than any of the other senses, we can expect that this child also has a sense of taste more certain, more fine, and more exquisitely tuned than civilized man's. This conjecture is founded on the unconquerable repugnance that he has for certain foods as well as on the natural appetites he has which lead him unfailingly to choose those foods that suit him.

Let him be shown the heavens, the green fields, the vast expanse of the earth, the works of Nature, he does not see anything in all that if there is nothing there to eat; and there you have the sole route by which external objects penetrate into his consciousness. It is astonishing how thoroughly this one idea absorbs him completely; he is always looking for something to eat, and he eats a lot. You might say his mind is in his stomach; it is his life center.

Shiny objects attract his attention; thus he likes anything that glitters; but he does not put any value on it. If shown some coins, he selects the shiniest, the whitest, the silver rather than the gold or copper; but I have seen him readily prefer a walnut to all these metals.

Our wild boy is ticklish, and he likes to be tickled, especially when he has eaten well or when he is in bed. When someone stops tickling him, he grasps their hand to get them to continue. He has a very pleasant laugh.

Consigned by nature to instinct alone, this child performs only purely animal functions: he has no knowledge whatever of those artificial passions or those conventional needs which become as demanding as natural needs: his desires do not exceed his physical needs. The only blessings he knows in the universe are nourishment, rest, and independence. Age has not at all developed that impetuous passion which torments and perpetuates all living beings; he has not yet experienced the sentiment of love.

All these details and many others that we could add establish that this child is not totally without intelligence, reflection, or reasoning; however, we are obliged to say that in all those cases where it is not a matter of meeting his natural needs or of satisfying his appetite, we find only purely animal function: if he has sensations, they do not give rise to ideas. One would say that there is no connection between his mind and his body, and that he reflects on nothing; consequently, he has no discernment, no imagination, no memory.

When he is flattered and caressed, this young man is sweet and complacent; if he is signaled to approach he does so.

He seems insensitive to expressions of affection; he does not know what it is to be caressed. While not wicked, he is not good, for he is unaware of both. He never does a mischievous or spiteful act, like children of his age; his caretaker has never seen him do anything of the sort.

If a hand is extended, he puts out his own, but he withdraws it brusquely, like a monkey; when on the contrary he is made impatient, when he is provoked, he makes movements of frenzy and anger. At the same time he lets out cries that announce his vexation, and occasionally skillfully bites those who are the cause of his rage.

The young Aveyronnais is naturally distrustful and on his guard unless he thinks the people around him are indifferent to him. If he is afraid of something, he throws himself in the arms of his caretaker and pushes him urgently toward his room, where he tries to close himself in and remain alone. He likes solitude a great deal; crowds irritate him and make him uncomfortable and temperamental; he avoids them as much as possible. When he is alone, he is happy to sleep, for he has nothing to do after he has eaten, and he almost never plays by himself; he does not even know what recreation is.

shock treatment, recalling Victor's terror when they had once walked along the parapet of the Paris observatory.

I soon found the occasion of a most violent fit, which was, I believe, caused by resumption of our lessons. Seizing the moment when his sensory functions were not yet suspended, I violently threw open the window of his room, which was on the fifth floor overlooking some boulders directly below. I approached him with every appearance of anger and grabbing him forcibly by the hips I held him out of the window, his head facing directly down toward the bottom of the chasm. After some seconds I drew him in again. He was pale, covered with a cold sweat, his eyes were wet with tears, and he still trembled a little, which I believed was the effect of his fear. I led him to the form boards, I made him gather up all the cards and replace them all. This was done, very slowly to be sure, and badly rather than well, but at least without impatience. Afterwards he went and threw himself on his bed and wept copiously.

This was the first time, at least to my knowledge, that he shed tears.

On June 17, 1801, in a summary of his progress, Itard returns to the broader philosophical issues that this metaphysical experiment undertook to clarify.

—In behalf of socialization he concludes, "That man is inferior to a large number of animals in the pure state of nature, a state of nullity and barbarism that has been falsely painted in the most seductive colors; a state in which the individual, deprived of the characteristic faculties of his kind, pitifully hangs on without intelligence and without feelings, a precarious life reduced to bare animal functions."

—In behalf of acquired ideas, "That the moral superiority said to be *natural* to man is only the result of civilization, which raises him above other animals by a great and powerful force."

—In behalf of a critical period for language acquisition, "That this imitative force, whose purpose is the education of his organs and especially the apprenticeship of speech, and which is very energetic and active during the first years of his life, wanes rapidly with age, with

isolation, and with all the causes which tend to blunt nervous sensitivity."

—In behalf of social reinforcers, "That in the most isolated savage as in the most highly civilized man, there exists a constant relation between ideas and needs; that the increasing multiplicity of the latter in the most civilized peoples should be considered as a great means of developing the human mind; so that a general proposition may be established, namely, that all causes, accidental, local or political, which tend to augment or diminish the number of our desires, necessarily contribute to extending or to narrowing the sphere of our knowledge and the domain of science, fine arts, and social industry."

—In behalf of individualized instruction, "That in the present state of our knowledge of physiology, the progress of education can and ought to be illumined by the light of modern medicine which, of all the natural sciences, can help most powerfully toward the perfection of the human species by detecting the organic and intellectual peculiarities of each individual and determining there from what education ought to do for him and what society can expect from him."

They continued to work for another four and a half years. In general, Victor was not socialized enough to commit antisocial acts; yet these would seem to be necessary if he was to acquire notions of justice and injustice in the absence of language. Like most parents, Itard used punishment to achieve this end. Originally Victor would help himself to food in the kitchen whenever he was hungry. Itard chastised him whenever he was caught in the act, and so Victor learned to steal with cunning what he had formerly taken openly. This gave Itard the opportunity to steal back; he would expropriate a coveted apple that the boy had earned and eat it in front of him; or he would surreptitiously empty Victor's pockets of provisions the boy had hid-

den there. Gradually Victor learned to take only what was explicitly his, though Itard was unsure of the cause. He drew a distinction between fear of punishment and disinterested moral motives:

In order to clear up this doubt and to obtain a less ambiguous result, I thought I ought to test my pupil's moral reactions by submitting him to another kind of injustice. . . . I chose a day for this truly painful experience when, after keeping Victor occupied for over two hours with our instructional procedures, I was satisfied both with his obedience and his intelligence, and had only praises and rewards to lavish on him. . . . But what was his astonishment when . . . he saw me suddenly assume a severe and menacing expression, rub out with all the outward signs of displeasure what I had just praised and applauded, scatter his books and cards into all corners of the room, and finally seize him by the arm and drag him violently toward a dark closet that had sometimes been used as his prison at the beginning of his stay in Paris. He allowed himself to be taken along quietly until he reached the threshold of the door. There, suddenly abandoning his usual attitude of obedience, he wedged himself with his feet and hands between the door posts, and resisted me vigorously, which delighted me so much the more because it was entirely new to him, and because he had always been ready to submit to similar punishments when merited and had never before refused to submit for a single moment, even with the slightest hesitation. I insisted, nevertheless, in order to see how far he would carry his resistance, and I tried to lift him from the ground with all my force in order to drag him into the closet. This last attempt excited all his fury. Outraged with indignation and red with anger, he struggled in my arms so violently that my efforts were fruitless for some moments; but finally, feeling himself giving in to the rule of force, he fell back upon the last resource of the weak and flew at my hand, leaving deep tooth-marks there. . . . It was a very legitimate act of vengeance; it was incontestable proof that the feeling of justice and injustice, that eternal basis of the social order, was no longer foreign to the heart of my pupil. In giving him this feeling, or rather in provoking its development, I had succeeded in raising the wild man to the full stature of moral man by means of the most pronounced of his characteristics and the most noble of his attributes.

In taking stock of Victor's moral development, Itard had to list on the debit side Victor's unattenuated egoism and his failure to show any evidence of pity. What troubled the teacher most, however, was his pupil's explosive and unsocialized sexuality. With young women, Victor seemed caught in a conflict between approach and avoidance. Itard recounts an incident:

I have seen him in the company of women trying to relieve his uneasiness by sitting beside one of them and gently pinching her hand, her arms, and her knees until, feeling his restless desires increased instead of calmed by these odd caresses, and seeing no relief from his painful emotions in sight, he suddenly changed his attitude and petulantly pushed away the woman whom he had sought with some eagerness. Then he turned without interruption to another woman, with whom he behaved in the same way.... These amorous demonstrations ended, as did all the others, with a feeling of annoyance which made him repulse the object of his passing fancy.

The teacher's conflicting emotions are clear at the end of his final report on the wild boy:

I did not doubt that if I had dared to reveal to this young man the secret of his restlessness and the aim of his desires, he would have reaped incalculable benefits. But, on the other hand, supposing I had been permitted to try such an experiment, should I not have been afraid to reveal a need to our savage which he would have sought to satisfy as publicly as his other wants and which would have led him to acts of revolting indecency? Intimidated by the possibility of such a result, I was obliged to stop at this point and once more to resign myself to seeing my hopes fade away, like so many other ones, before an unforeseen obstacle.

Significantly, Itard's report and, so far as we know, his program of education end on this note.

In summarizing what he had been unable to accomplish, Itard wrote:

First, as a result of the almost complete incapacity of the organs of hearing and speech, the education of this young man is still incomplete and must always remain so; second, by reason of their long inaction, the in-tellectual faculties are developing slowly and painfully, and this development, which in children growing up in civilized surroundings is the natural fruit of time and circumstances, is here the slow and laborious result of an intense training in which the most powerful methods are used to obtain the smallest effects; third, the emotional faculties, equally slow in emerging from their long torpor, are subordinated to a profound egoism, and puberty, instead of turning these emotions outward, seems to have expressed itself strongly only to prove that if there exists a relation between the needs of man's senses and the affection of his heart, then this sympathetic agreement is, like most great and generous notions, the happy fruit of education.

Finally, he summarized what his program of education had been able to achieve with Victor:

First, the improvement of his sight and touch and the new gratifications of his sense of taste have, by multiplying the sensations and ideas of our savage, contributed powerfully to the development of his intellectual faculties; second, when we consider the full extent of this development, we find, among other real improvements, that he has both a knowledge of the conventional value of the symbols of thought and the power of applying this knowledge by naming objects, their qualities, and their actions. This has led to an extension of the pupil's relations with the people around him, to his ability to express his wants to them, to receive orders from them, and to effect a free and continual exchange of thoughts with them; third, in spite of his immoderate taste for the freedom of the open country and his indifference to most of the pleasures of social life, Victor is aware of the care taken of him, susceptible to fondling and affection, sensitive to the pleasure of doing things well, ashamed of his mistakes, and repentant of his outbursts.

The official evaluation of the merits of Itard's program of instruction, solicited from the French Institute by the minister of the interior, had this to say:

[This class of the Institute] acknowledges that it was impossible for the instructor to put in his lessons, exercises, and experiments more intelligence, sagacity, patience, and courage; and that if he has not achieved greater success, it must be attributed not to any lack of zeal or talent but to the imperfection of the organs of the subject upon which he worked.

Nevertheless, Victor's education was abandoned. The ministry allocated 150 francs a year to Madame Guérin for her efforts and care, and the young man went to live with her in a nearby house belonging to the Institute. When the naturalist J. J. Virey visited him there nearly a decade later, he found him "fearful, half-wild, and unable to learn to speak, despite all the efforts that were made." Victor of Aveyron died in that house, in his forties, in the year 1828.

What did Victor finally prove about the nature of man? Some psychologists and psychiatrists, from the 1800's to the present, contend that he was congenitally retarded or, alternatively, an autistic child. In that case he proves nothing —except how self-sufficient such children can be. But a careful reading of Itard's reports on Victor's education rules out these diagnoses. We must conclude, then, that man depends on society not only for morality and communication but even for the most rudimentary discriminations, concepts, and skills. Social isolation is disastrous, and if it is prolonged, its effects are in large part irreversible. Man outside of society is an ignoble savage. We must finally have a renewed respect for Itard's empiricist philosophy and conclude with him:

"It is only in the heart of society that man can attain the pre-eminent position that nature has reserved for him. Cast upon this globe without physical strength or innate ideas, he is incapable by himself of following the fundamental laws of his nature which call him to the first rank of the animal kingdom. Without civilization he would be one of the feeblest and least intelligent of animals."

Harlan Lane is chairman of the Department of Psychology at Northeastern University. This article is adapted from The Wild Boy of Aveyron, *which will be published early this year by Harvard University Press.*

"*Greatness Lies in Doing Little Things Well*"

Ernest Bloch was speaking about his lifework, writing music.
The same affection for detail is in his photographic work—
a recently rediscovered record of another time, another place

ALL PRINTS: ERIC JOHNSON

Bloch, at right, and his cousin, Leon Goetschel, in the Haute-Savoie, 1912

A self-portrait, Brussels, 1897

*E*rnest Bloch, a major composer of this century, has been called a "romantic in an antiromantic age," and his music is known for its rich harmonic effects and emotional intensity. Born in Geneva in 1880, he emigrated in 1916 to the United States, where he made his reputation as a composer of chamber music and suites for voice and orchestra, a Jewish Cycle that paid tribute to his religious heritage, and *America*, a symphonic rhapsody that celebrated his adopted land. Partly as a relief from his work, Bloch pursued another art—photography—for nearly sixty years, leaving at his death in 1959 some five thousand negatives that are now in the hands of Eric Johnson, a West Coast photographer who made the prints in this portfolio. They reveal the composer's affectionate eye, as well as his skill with a camera.

Many of these pictures were taken in Bloch's beloved countryside around Geneva: at Satigny, where he lived in the years before he came to America, and in the French Haute-Savoie region south of Geneva, where he often took long hikes. At Satigny, he photographed members of his family (overleaf 2 and 5) and a neighbor who sold mushrooms she picked in the woods nearby (6). On a hike to Mont Salève, in the Haute-Savoie, Bloch, using a tripod and time-delaying device, took a picture of himself and his cousin having a leisurely picnic, above. On the mountain he photographed his hiking companions (3), a peasant family outside an inn (1), and a group at the summit (7). Some twenty years later, again in the Haute-Savoie, he shot a characteristically tranquil panorama of hills, trees, and shining rooftops (4). Although Bloch's music was often tumultuously dramatic, his photographs express a more peaceful side of this gifted man. —P.F.

1. *The photographer, back row center, and his son Ivan, front row second from left, with a peasant family on Mont Salève, 1912*

2. *The Bloch children, Suzanne and Lucienne, left front, and Ivan, second from right, with their cousins at Satigny, 1912*

3. *Hiking companions, including Leon Goetschel, left front, on Mont Salève, 1912*

4. Châtel, Haute-Savoie, 1935

5. *Leon Goetschel, his wife, Helen, and her mother at Satigny, 1912*

6. Mme. Bertrand, Satigny, 1912

7. *Ivan Bloch, at left, patting a goat, and Bloch, at far right, on Mont Salève, 1912*

Eric Partridge
and the
Underworld of Language

At eighty-one he is the Godfather of slang

There is a desk near the entrance to the Reading Room of the British Museum where one man has sat for forty years, writing dictionaries. Though regulations do not allow anyone to reserve a desk in the Reading Room, a scarf, a small battered suitcase, and a shabby felt hat lie here, at desk K.1, with the casual authority of regalia. This is Eric Partridge's desk. Only illness and World War II have ever displaced him.

The Reading Room has always had its legends. Attendants will point out where Shaw sat, where Lenin plotted the overthrow of an empire, and where Marx questioned the foundations of the world. Now Partridge, a lean, desiccated shape crouched over his papers, is the last legend among the scholars, refugees, and revolutionaries who have come and gone under the museum's great dome. Last year, at K.1, he celebrated his eighty-first birthday.

There will never be anything like him again. He is the one twentieth-century man who has found it possible to bestride language, literature, slang, changing fashion, and the current sum of knowledge. It is an achievement that belongs more to the springtime of the Renaissance or the dusty college libraries of the eighteenth century. Edmund Wilson called him the "Word

King"; H. L. Mencken and Raymond Chandler sought his advice. Dictionaries, of course, will get written after Partridge, but they will be the products of regiments of scholars. He is the last of Samuel Johnson's species.

There is more to his achievement than this. By trafficking in the strange waters of slang, Partridge began to change something as fundamental as our attitude toward language itself. The fantasy still survives, preserved by some scholars, that there is such a thing as a perfect language, immutable and correct. Partridge, by treating slang as the subject of serious academic study, made it clear that language is the speech of men, and that only this underwrites its rules. "All writing is based on speech," he says, "and not the other way round. Language is not created in a laboratory, but by people and for people. It's the spirit of a people."

In every library in the English-speaking world there is one reference shelf that all writers eventually consult. The books here begin with the Oxford English Dictionary and proceed magisterially through Roget's *Thesaurus* and Fowler's *Modern English Usage*. This is the shrine to the language itself. To see one's work added to this reference shelf is an accomplishment of legendary proportion. Partridge's *A Dictionary of Slang and Unconventional English*, his etymological dictionary, *Origins*, and *Usage and Abusage* all appear here. At

present from K.1, where his hunt for what Cowper called "the panting syllables" has led him "to Gaul, to Greece, and into Noah's Ark," Partridge's energies, at the beginning of his ninth decade, are directed to adding *A Dictionary of Catch Phrases* to that shelf.

"It's been an industrous life, pursued by a lunatic," says Partridge. "What would I tell a young man? For God's sake, not to start it, otherwise he'll break his heart."

Partridge looks like one of those crabby old-timers who give misdirections to posses in Westerns. As he stands alone on the steps of the museum during one of his breaks, smoking cigarettes down to the last millimeter, he seems to be looking for a hitching post to lean on. His few teeth are yellowed by a habit that he has now reduced to twenty cigarettes a day. He is leaner than Jimmy Stewart.

If his achievement seems odd in the twentieth century, so does his life style. He lives alone in North London, in a single room, an old man's room with medicine at the bedside. A few years ago he sold his library of twenty-five hundred volumes to help keep his wife, whose health is failing, at a private nursing home in the West Country near their daughter. He no longer has a complete set of his own books. The room is in a house belonging to a friend, an accountant. Partridge has lived here since 1972. Suitcases stacked under a small table give the impression of a man passing through.

Over the mantelpiece is a birthday card from his nine-year-old grandchild. It begins, "Now You Are Eighty." Partridge picks it up and says wryly, "Deadly realists, children. I keep it there to remind myself."

For the past forty years Partridge's life has been structured to outwit time. His routine is meticulous; disrupting it even for a luncheon appointment sends ripples across the whole week.

Every morning he gets up at 7:30, shaves, and takes public transportation to the museum. He gets there at nine o'clock, when the doors open. If he is too early, he waits on the underground platform of the Holborn Tube Station. His London has shrunk to a small triangle between the tube station, the museum, and the small Italian restaurants of Bloomsbury, where he eats lunch alone. Until last year, when illness interrupted his regimen, he stayed in the museum until it closed in the evening. He now leaves at 2 P.M.

In the afternoon he returns to his room and spends an hour on his mail. ("The number of people who write to me! They think, 'Poor old Partridge, he's got nothing to do.' Most of them could get their information from a dictionary. They've got no idea that I've got a living to make.") He then reads until supper, after which he reads again. He goes to bed each night at 10:30.

"It all sounds terribly pedestrian," says Partridge, "but it does save time. A routine is an imaginative use of time. By having one, I save myself strain. It's an aid to work. People say to me, 'Mr. Partridge, aren't you interested in art?' Of course I am, but I can't afford the time. I'm social in my tendencies, but I've had to cut them out. I attend my club, the Savile, every Wednesday at lunchtime. I used to lunch and dine there, but I've given up the dinners. I was no good the next day for my work. I'm not a recluse, but there's not the time. I'm sometimes asked to give public lectures. I always decline them. They're so disruptive. They take up so much time."

Time is a crucial element in his conversation: "I used to be a devotee of the cinema until a few years ago. I don't go at all now. It's so hard on the eyes. I tell you, one has to give things up. I used to go to Wimbledon for a magazine every year until ten years ago. How the pieces got used, I never knew. I mean, they were quite decently written." He grins mischievously. "But I don't go to Wimbledon now. There isn't time." He adds almost with wonder, as though speaking of a quite different person, "And I used to be mad about tennis. Crackers. Bonkers. What have you." The lexicographer in him never sleeps.

Talking to him, one occasionally catches a glimpse of the nonlexicographical Partridge, the man with small, private enthusiasms. He had long hero-worshiped the famous tennis player of the thirties, Alice Marble, and had said so often enough in his tennis reports. The one day she wrote to him. "I was delighted to get the letter," he says. "Who wouldn't be, to get a letter from Alice Marble?" He pauses for a long time, then adds, "Particularly as it was so literate."

But mostly he thinks about words, though in a distinctly unacademic way. In the preface to his *English*, which he subtitled *A Course for Human Beings*, he wrote, "I have been much concerned with English ever since I could say 'No.'" His frequent earthy expletives remind one of the World War I infantryman he was. He does not suffer fools gladly.

All this is reflected in his career. Except for two years as a university lecturer, it has been conducted entirely outside the sleek groves of academe. ("I hear that's well-paid now," he says, grinning wickedly through his yellow teeth. "They get this wonderful superannuation.") There is an unmistakable tension between him and the academic world. In spite of the fact that sixteen of his books are in print and American reprint houses can provide copies of another twenty-six, Partridge has received only one honorary degree, a D.Lit. from Queens Island University.

"It was the first they'd ever given for services to the language," he says. "I'm Doctor Partridge now. I got that in 1965. Very few people know it. If you keep quiet, nobody finds out."

Partridge thinks of himself as a freelance writer. Thus one of the most distinguished lexicographers of our day is not averse to turning his hand to something like *Name Your Child*, a small glossary of names. "Little Bread and butter job," he says airily.

"Since 1931 I've been a writer," he explains. "Not an author. A free-lance writer. The official description on the Inland Revenue forms is author. But I'm a lexicographer, not an author. I keep putting down 'writer.' It's childish, I suppose, but nothing's fun if you're not childish."

For all his sales he is not a rich man. "It's a damned precarious business, this. I suppose I'm a bit above the breadline, but you see, I've never written textbooks. That's where the money is. If I write for anybody in particular, I write for the public, the educated general public. They're the salt of the earth."

Partridge's has, in fact, probably been the strangest literary career of our time. He has made a living from the language, not be erecting it along the trellis of his own imagination but through recording its forms, by being its only living index. "I do sometimes look back on it all and laugh," he says. "Scholars have asked me why I don't work with a team as editor in chief. They ask me why I take on these immense tasks. My only answer to them is that I prefer to make my own mistakes. I'm one of those independent cusses who don't work well with other people."

Partridge takes just one week's holiday a year, always alone and always at the end of September, at a Catholic college on the borders of Derbyshire and Staffordshire. He has done this since just after World War II. He is not a Catholic, but a friend of his was once headmaster there. He walks on the nearby moors, talks to the priests, reads. "In the evenings I used to watch television," he says. "Not now. I value my eyesight too much. And they have color television, you know." There is something almost wistful in his voice.

The past five years have been taken up with reading for his *Dictionary of Catch Phrases*. Now, in the museum, he is writing it laboriously in longhand. At his elbow are heaps of notebooks containing his research. If his health holds up, he hopes to finish it in two years.

It has already taken him to some of the odder reaches of popular folklore and show business, all among the stacked books of the museum's Reading Room. It has also left him with a fervent admiration for Mae West, who, he has discovered, is his senior in age. " 'Beulah, peel me a grape'," Partridge says dreamily.

It is rare for anyone to originate a catch phrase. Occasionally a phrase is popular and then completely vanishes, only to reappear years later. "Where do we go from here?" began life as part of a popular song in America, and in the twenties was the sort of thing people said when they were leaving bars. In the past fifteen years it has reappeared in Britain, where it is useful in political, moral, or economic crises.

"My own particular favorite," he says, "is when someone asks you how you are. I then say, 'I don't know. I've been far too busy to ask.' " He sighs. "It's never caught on."

"There is no really satisfactory definition of a catch phrase," Partridge points out. "A flippant one is that it is a phrase that catches on and becomes popular. But so does a cliché. The irony is that a cliché can become a catch phrase, especially when it is used laughingly. It is all very difficult."

What has made him do it, then? What led to his regimen, to this loneliness of the long-distance lexicographer?

Partridge was born in New Zealand, a farmer's son. Volunteering for the Australian forces after graduating, he found himself on the heights of Gallipoli, being fired upon by Turkish guns. Most men in the war probably dreamed of home or survival; Partridge dreamed of further education. "I remember saying to myself, 'Partridge, if you're one of

---

PARTRIDGE ON USAGE:
A Pride of Prejudices

Ambiguity springs from woolly and muddled thinking; from a hasty fitting of words to the thought; from ignorance of the order of words; from defective punctuation; and from a multiplicity of minor causes.

That ambiguity which springs from vague and muddled thinking . . . is ambiguity on a large scale and is especially to be found in political speeches, in the words of publicists, and in the writings of such numerous vulgarizers as have failed to understand the views and thoughts of those whom they seek to vulgarize.

Nicknames are permissible among friends, and, for the great or the famous or the notorious, among all men (and women); but in writing . . . they are to be avoided. Gossip writers affect them, for nicknames in a gossip column give the impression that the writer knows intimately the person nicknamed or is at least in the enviable position of knowing the name if not the person. . . . There is an increasing tendency in American businesses . . . to call nearly everyone by his first name or by a nickname. It may produce a friendly atmosphere but it does not keep John from firing Charlie.

Plurals, Snob. Big-game hunters are in the habit of speaking of *a herd of antelope* or *giraffe* or *elephant*, *a troop of lion, a crash of rhinoceros*. . . .

This sort of thing is all very well . . . on safari. . . . But when, at the zoo, you hear a man, who doesn't know the difference between a jaguar and a cougar, say to his son, aged seven, "Just look at those two lion, Willie!," you feel that snobbery has become a symptom of "the larger lunacy."

—FROM *Usage and Abusage*, 1947

---

those lucky buggers who get through this, you're going to Oxford.' There were something like eleven hundred men in a battalion then. I was one of twenty-odd who got through. So I went to Oxford."

In the early twenties he became a university lecturer in England. He lasted two years. "The second year, to my horror and disgust I found I was repeating

---

myself. I couldn't face it, so I got out."

The lexicographer was still unhatched. With a friend he set up a small publishing firm, bringing out H. E. Bates's first novel. With his usual realism he also published himself: "It was a book of short stories under the name Corrie Dennison. Where the hell I got that from, I don't know. The book had two hundred and fifty-six pages. I wrote the whole thing in four and a half weeks. I also wrote a novel. I'm damned if I remember the pseudonym for that. Bloody bad novel. Plague knocks out ninety-nine per cent of the male population of England. I had to make play with the fact that the remainder were, shall we say, much sought after by the ladies. But I had too much facility. I could just sit down and write. Just like that. I could see I wasn't going to be much good."

During his publishing years he reprinted, with a commentary, Francis Grose's *Dictionary of the Vulgar Tongue*, first published in 1785. It appealed to the scholar and the explorer in Partridge. "Now that, I suppose, really did get me hooked, because it was such new ground. Nobody had ever tackled it before." There was a century and a half to account for, and words and phrases to be hunted back long before Grose, who had, in any event, declared roundly that slang was only "A nasty name for a nasty thing."

The publishers Routledge and Kegan Paul read the book and commissioned Partridge to do a history of slang. He left his company, extricated himself from fiction, and settled down to free-lance writing. It was the worst possible time for it, with the Depression lurching across England. But he survived, and the history became the two-volume dictionary.

It is difficult now to conceive of the kind of reception the dictionary received. Partridge's own father professed himself disgusted when he first saw the book. "He was horrified that I should have written on so low a subject," says Partridge. "Just before he died one of my brothers asked him what he thought of me now, and he said, 'Well, he seems to have made a success of it.' " Women would turn to Partridge at parties (apparently time did not run so fleetly in 1937) and ask him whether he thought it was quite nice to have written such a book. Very gently he would reply that, no, it wasn't nice, but that he was just a recorder.

Chesterton once wrote, "Good slang is the one stream of poetry which is constantly flowing." Partridge himself had seen slang evolve during the First World War, and he loved its excitement and novelty. But nobody before him had thought of making it the subject of serious academic study. "You see, it wasn't considered reputable for a scholar. He could write an essay in a lighter moment perhaps." Partridge pauses. "I was a ruddy pioneer, I suppose. It didn't strike me like that then."

Before him, slang was a kind of popular mystery. Most people could offer some sort of garbled explanation for its phrases. But Partridge hunted them back. His search took him to strange places, to long-forgotten wars, to colonizations even the colonizers had forgotten. The Egyptian campaigns of the late nineteenth century produced "bint," or prostitute, from "saida Bint," literally the Arabic for "good-day girl." The two world wars brought whole chapters of slang. Even the Korean War left "gook," "chop chop," and, from the forbidding landscape, the melancholy poetry of "the hills are closing round him"—he is becoming very odd.

His was the first readable dictionary since Johnson's. Writing a dictionary alone, a man can allow himself the humor of idiosyncratic definitions. Thus in the seventh edition, published in 1971, Partridge defines the Mod of the mid 1960's as "a teenager unable to afford a motorcycle and doing his damndest with a scooter."

Some of the joy in a slang dictionary comes from seeing serious etymological definitions applied to such phrases as "To put one's balls in a knot"—which Partridge defines as "Low equivalent of Standard English, to put one's nose out of joint. Ca. 1930."

Since the subject is so new, one has a whiff of the sheer exhilaration of etymology that standard dictionaries no longer provide. Partridge succeeded in establishing an etymology for "phony." He traced it back to "fawney" of the late eighteenth century, especially in the "fawney-dropping trick" which con men played. A man would pretend to find a silver ring in front of his victim. It would actually be silver-plated. Taking advantage of gullibility and greed, he would sell it to the victim for less than its supposed, but ten times its real, value. With a further wild leap, Partridge traced this back to Irish Gaelic *fáinne*, a ring. "That's even got into the Shorter Oxford now," he says with some smugness. "Of course you can't acknowledge sources in a dictionary. I'm used to being used."

His greatest coup was with "tanner," slang for the English sixpence. "Now that was a real mystery," he says. "It had baffled etymologists for over a century. But then I remembered that the seventeenth-century underworld word for a sixpence was 'a simon.' Suddenly one day, sometime before the Second World War, it came to me. I just sat down and thought, and it didn't require much thought. It was in the New Testament, 'He lodgeth with one Simon, a tanner.' It was a combination of sheer luck and what some people call misguided ingenuity. But you couldn't get a clearer run than that."

It is tempting to think of Partridge, notebook in hand, creeping through the fog of London's East End to collect information for his books on slang (especially for his later works on underworld jargon). However, he has always done 90 per cent of his research in the British Museum. "Remember that ninety-five per cent of criminals are just bloody stupid," he says. "It's the people on the fringe who are most helpful—beggars, social workers. I got a lot of my American criminal slang from the Kefauver Report on Crime. It couldn't have been more official, but it was very valuable."

After the dictionary was published, Partridge began to acquire a network of informants. They range from the late Evelyn Waugh to "Albert Petch of Bournemouth, tireless gleaner and tenacious rememberer." They are acknowledged in the preface of each edition. "A lot of tramps wrote to me," he says. "I'd give them a drink or two in a pub." But there was always the risk, particularly in printed books, that the author had actually made up his own slang. "One convict told me he needed a dictionary to read Raymond Chandler. I asked Chandler about this and he admitted making words up. But some American lexicographers still quote him."

He now has some twenty regular correspondents, scattered all over the English-speaking world. "They've always written in to me. If they're no good I send them a thank-you letter. If they show promise and some critical sense,

STATEMENT OF OWNERSHIP, MANAGEMENT, AND CIRCULATION

(Act of August 12, 1970; Section 3685, Title 39, U.S. Code)

1. Title of publication: HORIZON
2. Date of filing: October 1, 1975
3. Frequency of issue: quarterly
   a. Annual subscription price: $26.00
4. Location of known office of publication: 1221 Avenue of the Americas, N.Y., N.Y. 10020
5. Location of the headquarters or general business offices of the publishers: 1221 Avenue of the Americas, N.Y., N.Y. 10020
6. Names and addresses of Publisher, Editor, and Managing Editor: Publisher, Marjorie C. Dyer, 1221 Avenue of the Americas, N.Y., N.Y. 10020; Editor: Shirley Tomkievicz, 1221 Avenue of the Americas, N.Y., N.Y. 10020; Managing Editor: James F. Fixx, 1221 Avenue of the Americas, N.Y., N.Y. 10020
7. Owner: American Heritage Publishing Co., Inc., 1221 Avenue of the Americas, N.Y., N.Y. 10020. Names and addresses of stockholders owning or holding 1 per cent or more of total amount of stock of American Heritage Publishing Co., Inc.: McGraw-Hill, Inc., 1221 Avenue of the Americas, N.Y., N.Y. 10020 (100 per cent)
8. Known bondholders, mortgagees, and other security holders owning or holding 1 per cent or more of total amount of bonds, mortgages, or other securities: none

9. For optional completion by publishers mailing at the regular rates (Section 132.121, Postal Service Manual), 39 U.S.C. 3626 provides in pertinent part: "No person who would have been entitled to mail matter under former section 4359 of this title shall mail such matter at the rates provided under this subsection unless he files annually with the Postal Service a written request for permission to mail matter at such rates."

In accordance with the provisions of this statute, I hereby request permission to mail the publication named in Item 1 at the reduced postage rates presently authorized by 39 U.S.C. 3626.

Marjorie C. Dyer, Publisher

10. For completion by nonprofit organizations authorized to mail at special rates: not applicable

11. Extent and nature of circulation:

	Average No. Copies Each Issue During Preceding 12 Months	Actual No. of Copies of Single Issue Published Nearest to Filing Date
A. Total No. Copies Printed (Net Press Run)	111,500	108,000
B. Paid Circulation		
1. Sales through dealers and carriers, street vendors, and counter sales	800	700
2. Mail Subscriptions	101,400	98,300
C. Total Paid Circulation	102,200	99,000
D. Free Distribution by Mail, Carrier, or Other Means, Samples, Complimentary, and Other Free Copies	5,000	6,700
E. Total Distribution (Sum of C and D)	107,200	105,700
F. Copies Not Distributed		
1. Office Use, Leftover, Unaccounted, Spoiled After Printing	4,300	2,300
2. Returns From News Agents	—	—
G. Total (Sum of E and F—should equal net press run shown in A)	111,500	108,000

I certify that the statements made by me above are correct and complete.

Marjorie C. Dyer, Publisher

Confessions of a Lone Lexicographer

For some perhaps not too obscure reason my name has become synonymous with lexicography, even though several of my books are not strictly or entirely lexicographical. Admittedly, however, my three largest books are dictionaries: *A Dictionary of Slang and Unconventional English*, first published in 1937; *A Dictionary of the Underworld*, which appeared in 1950; and *Origins: An Etymological Dictionary of Modern English*, 1958.

It was these three works that prompted a scholar friend of mine to ask why I undertook such exhausting tasks instead of heading a team of collaborators. "First of all," I told him, "I prefer to make my own mistakes. Also, you know the old saw, 'So many men, so many opinions.' But have you considered the equally indisputable fact, 'So many men, so many styles'? Would any of those dictionaries have been as readable if they had been written by, say, six people? Wouldn't some jarring discrepancies and irritating infelicities have resulted? Moreover, wouldn't the tempo and the character of the writing have varied in disconcerting ways?"

All the same, however grand one's reasons may seem to oneself, it's more satisfactory to be honest than complacent. The underlying, and overriding, reason I've written most of my books by myself is that I *am* a loner. An even more compelling reason is that there are so few people, scholars included, who know much about catch phrases, slang, or cant—the convenient scholarly name for the language of the underworld.

This dearth of potential collaborators and assistants is a serious matter: of the "potentials," only a small proportion would be available at all; of those available, every single one would need to be trained—a process that would take months; and as the work progressed, they would frequently be descending on me to solve this or that problem. I not only hate to boss people; I'm also an impatient fellow. They would drive me crazy long before I drove them crazy.

There are disadvantages in working alone. The one inescapable risk is a severe illness or a grave disablement. A lesser risk is inferior proofreading; every writer tends to read what he knows should be there. I can only hope that in the work-in-progress I don't pass over some cataclysmic and painfully embarrassing slip of the pen.

That work-in-progress is *A Dictionary of Catch Phrases*, and I should caution potential readers. By the very nature of the subject, the phrases can be extremely earthy and some may be frankly bawdy. For example, there is the phrase "Hullo! hullo! hullo!" which is the traditional British policeman's monitory comment on an untoward incident or situation. It becomes a catch phrase when it is used allusively. A neat example of such allusion occurs in the story of the young policeman who returns home unexpectedly one day, finds his wife in bed with three men, and mildly exclaims, "Hullo, hullo, hullo!" His wife thereupon bursts into tears and reproaches the clumsy fellow with the classic words, "Darling, you didn't say hullo to *me!*"

Thus *A Dictionary of Catch Phrases* may not please the prudish. But my attitude has been scholarly, therefore almost clinical; and the treatment will be, I like to believe, not merely humane but entirely human.

—ERIC PARTRIDGE

I'm very nice to them. I might even send them one of my books."

The dictionary is now in its seventh edition. Partridge hopes to complete an eighth. "When I'm dead I won't give a damn what happens to it, but not as long as I'm compos, I suppose there must be a few people who could do it." He leans across the table and says in a completely matter-of-fact voice, without pride, "Mind you, I don't know who they are."

One can appreciate Partridge's achievement only if it is set against conventional etymological dictionaries. An etymologist always has earlier dictionaries to quote, or to disagree with. Partridge had little other than his curiosity, his erudition, and his eccentric reading. The greatest source of all, he recalls with awe, was a novel published by a man called James Curtis in 1937, *The Gilt Kid*, about the life of a young criminal. Nobody remembers *The Gilt Kid* now, except Partridge. He has a great loyalty to his sources.

The irony about the success of the slang dictionary is that Partridge, at eighty-one, feels that it is somewhat of an albatross around his neck: "One of the things I do resent is that I'm known as the bloke who wrote the slang book. I'm fond of it but my deeper interest was always in language, and inevitably in etymology. I didn't get interested in slang until the 1930's, and then only through a chain of circumstances."

"Like being commissioned to write it," he adds dryly.

He is proudest of his etymological dictionary, *Origins*, which has sold only some seven thousand copies since it was published in 1958, nothing akin to the scale of the slang dictionary. "It only costs ninety shillings," says Partridge. "Absolute snip. My favorite book of the whole damned lot. It was something I'd always wanted to do." It was also academically respectable. In his small room in London he still has a copy.

He measures his success by odd yardsticks. Two years ago he was given a shelf in the north library of the Reading Room to keep his assorted notebooks. It is a privilege sometimes temporarily extended to an important visiting scholar, but never to a resident. "The final benison," sighs Partridge happily.

Once he came to his desk a few minutes late and found someone else there. "I told him I'd been sitting there for forty years. He said, 'There is no rule.' He was a real Prussian. He refused to move. I told him I'd see to it he didn't sit there again.

"I got one of the attendants to put my books there the next day before the Reading Room opened. I came half a minute late. On purpose. The German was there, boggling at my papers. I said, very politely, 'Excuse me,' and sat down. You have to use your brains, my dear man." Partridge grins, a long, smoke-blackened grin: it had been a famous victory.

At eight-one he has lost none of his grim humor. "Yes, I hope to die with my boots on. But not at K.1. It would be such a bloody nuisance for them."

Byron Rogers is an English journalist who writes for the Daily Telegraph Magazine.

Love Among the Ruins

Antony's affair with Cleopatra was, at the start,
statecraft spiced with pleasure.
It turned into infatuation poisoned by statecraft,
and then came the dénouement

Brutus called him a "lover of great deeds," but alas for Mark Antony, he is best remembered for affections of a different sort. On the afternoon of September 2, 31 B.C., in the Bay of Actium off the west coast of Greece, the brave and vaunting Antony, co-ruler of the Roman world, fixed himself forever in human memory as the most besotted lover in history. That day, locked in combat for supremacy of the Roman world, Antony abandoned his ships and his troops and set off in hot pursuit of Queen Cleopatra as she sailed away from the battle. Antony's sailors surrendered, his leaderless army laid down its arms. His hated rival Octavian became the first emperor of Rome. In a singular act of blind frustration Antony had encompassed a singularly shattering ruin, and the story of it has bemused humankind ever since.

Well it might. For no other major episode in history has been shaped so decisively by the essentially private passion of love. Yet there has always been something amiss in the story. It is our common experience of love that arouses our suspicion, for love normally runs a course from hot to cool. With Antony, it began cool and ended in consuming passion. At its outset, Antony's affair with Cleopatra was chiefly statecraft spiced with pleasure. Not for years would it become infatuation poisoned by statecraft.

It is a curious anomaly. Shakespeare, following Plutarch, got around it by assuming—quite falsely—that from the

start Antony was more or less in Cleopatra's thrall. Even that left a problem—the sheer durability of Cleopatra's appeal. "Age cannot wither, nor custom stale her infinite variety," wrote Shakespeare by way of explanation. "Other women cloy the appetites they feed, but she makes hungry where most she satisfies." That was no doubt true, but it hardly explains why Cleopatra should

Cleopatra as the fateful mistress, portrayed by Theda Bara in 1917

finally enslave Antony ten years after she first became his mistress. To understand that, I think, we must depart from the arena of love and return to the loveless arena of power.

The story of Antony and Cleopatra began with a political predicament peculiar to Rome at that time: how to establish autocratic power on some sort of legitimate foundation in what was still, in theory, a republic. In 41 B.C., when the twenty-nine-year-old Antony summoned the twenty-four-year-old queen of Egypt to Tarsus and his bed, auto-

cratic power of the most commanding sort was his to enjoy. At the snap of his fingers, dynasties were made and unmade, treasure-troves emptied, legions raised, expeditions launched. Yet his power had always rested on only the shakiest of foundations.

Officially, Antony bore the title of triumvir, along with Caesar's sickly grandnephew Octavian, then twenty years old, and a third Roman named Lepidus, a makeweight of no consequence. Between them Antony and Octavian had divided up the Roman world, Octavian ruling the west and Antony taking the lion's share, the rich and docile Hellenized east. Only by the most transparent fiction could the Roman constitution legitimate their autocracy. In theory, the triumvirs bore a temporary commission from the Senate to reorganize the empire and restore the unrestorable republic. The fiction could not have deceived a child. Men obeyed the two triumvirs for one reason only: they were regarded as the heirs of the great Julius Caesar.

In that fact lies the measure of Caesar's greatness. His feats had been so extraordinary, his genius so towering, his personal glory so unexampled, that two men could rule the Roman world as autocrats because they were deemed the true heirs of his greatness. Men agreed that the swashbuckling Antony was Caesar's spiritual heir—his trusted lieutenant, the avenger of his death, the servant of his military glory. Unfortu-

By WALTER KARP

nately for Antony, Octavian was Caesar's legal heir—his posthumously adopted son and the bearer of his magical name. Antony, the spiritual heir, had no such tangible legitimacy, and unless he found its match, time would gnaw at his laurels and inexorably erode his power. From the moment he went east to rule his half of the world, his life became one long quest for legitimacy. The quest took him to Cleopatra, queen and pharaoh of Egypt.

The direction was all but inevitable. Historians have often asked why Antony did not invade Italy, conquer Octavian, and take supreme command. The question is naive. Caesar's spiritual heir could not wage war against Caesar's legal heir. It would have been treason to Caesar's memory, and it was upon his loyalty to Caesar's memory that Antony's power rested. He had to leave Octavian alone in the west and hope the young man would leave him alone in the east. There, Antony intended to put into practice a far-reaching plan for securing his power.

Characteristically, it had been Caesar's own plan for securing power. Beyond Rome's eastern frontier lay the redoubtable empire of the Parthians. To conquer and annex that empire, Caesar had believed, would be a feat of glory so grandiose that he would be hailed as Rome's second founder. Antony intended to do the same. If he could execute great Caesar's greatest military project, then power would be truly and permanently his.

Egypt beckoned Antony immediately. If he could draw upon its riches, he could carry out his vast scheme of conquest without hindrance from the meddlesome Octavian. Egypt, of course, meant Cleopatra, for she stood at the head of the most efficiently centralized autocracy in the world. If Cleopatra made "hungry where most she satisfied," the hunger in question was Antony's hunger for gold. But Cleopatra had other charms. She had been Caesar's mistress and the mother of his child. The idea of trumping Caesar's adopted son by championing his

blood son was ever-present in the Caesar-haunted brain of Antony. Hoping to secure the independence of her dynasty, Cleopatra fell in with Antony's plans and into his arms.

Sojourning with Antony in Alexandria during the winter of 41–40 B.C., Cleopatra discovered quickly enough that her Roman champion had one glaring weakness. Antony loved the noise and tumult of revelry and the ecstatic pleasures of victory. He loved great deeds, but he loved even more the celebration of them. To reign as king was Antony's fondest ambition, to ride in triumph his greatest joy.

He was not at all Cleopatra's infatuated lover. Leaving Alexandria in early 40 B.C., Antony did not see the queen for three and a half years. In the meantime, endless difficulties delayed his Parthian enterprise. Not until late 37 B.C. was he able to turn his attention to war. Accordingly, he summoned Cleo-

Antony as the fatuous lover

patra to his side once more. At Antioch, she promised to put Egypt's wealth at Antony's disposal. This time, however, she drove a hard bargain. She now understood that Antony's Parthian campaign was not the fruit of his overflowing ambition but a political necessity of the most exigent kind. In return for Egyptian gold, Cleopatra demanded large chunks of Roman territory for her dynasty. Antony had no choice but to agree. In fact, he was now embarked on a vicious cycle: the more dependent on Egypt he became, the less secure his support in Rome, the less secure his support

in the capital, the more dependent on Cleopatra he would become.

Antony was scarcely fretful. He fully expected to destroy the Parthians when, in March, 36 B.C., his great expeditionary force set out. Instead the nimble Parthian cavalry almost destroyed his army. Antony was never the same again. He still planned to conquer the Parthians, but it must have been more out of habit than conviction. His vainglory, hitherto an amusing vice, now became dangerous, and Cleopatra exploited it to further her own dynastic schemes. Antony might be a troubled Roman magistrate elsewhere in the world, but in Egypt he was a pharaoh's consort, the god Dionysus incarnate.

The implacable Octavian watched and waited. In 33 B.C. he felt strong enough to announce that he would not renew the triumvirate. On January 1, 32 B.C., Mark Antony, a god in Alexandria, became a private citizen in the Roman world. Octavian now compelled Antony to do what he had felt powerless to do in the noontime of his power—wage civil war against Caesar's legal heir.

Antony was a brave man and dauntless in battle. Yet even before the first clash of arms he was already beaten, not by Cleopatra's allure but by Caesar's haunting presence. He had failed in his quest for legitimacy; he had failed as the executor of Caesar's plans. He was now about to lose the great sustaining principle of his life: his belief that he above all others had been loyal to Caesar's memory. As civil war tensions mounted, a change came over Antony: the more he was forced to turn away from Caesar's memory, the more desperately he clung to Caesar's former mistress. In the months before the Battle of Actium he could not bear having Cleopatra out of his sight. In the dénouement at Actium, his infatuation for Cleopatra was not his downfall but merely the final straw: ultimately, it cost him his honor and his name. Posterity is only half right in remembering Antony as the man who encompassed his ruin for love. That love had been born in his political ruin, and in his ruin as a man.

High Noon for the Empire

In 1911, in Delhi, they staged a celebration
that would have made Cecil B. De Mille blush

By DAVID F. PHILLIPS

Indian subjects by the thousands prepare for Their Majesties' entrance to Delhi in 1911.

In 1911 in the old Mogul capital of Delhi, an extravaganza was held that can be called matchless. It was the coronation durbar of George V, king of England and emperor of India. Durbars—the gathering of chiefs to pay homage—were nothing new. Nawabs and samindars had held them for generations, and so had the British viceroys. In 1877, after Queen Victoria adopted the style and title of queen-empress of India, her viceroy, Lord Lytton, held a durbar in Delhi to proclaim her imperial sway. That durbar was the first imperial durbar, and the attendance of ruling princes from all over India was required. It was a very splendid occasion indeed.

When Edward VII succeeded his mother on the throne, another imperial durbar was held, on New Year's Day, 1903. Known as Lord Curzon's durbar, it was a far more magnificent occasion than Lord Lytton's, for Lord Curzon was aware of the importance of pomp and spectacle in governing India. "You will never rule the East," he said in 1904, "except through the heart."

Six years later, George V ascended the throne. As duke of York and, later, Prince of Wales, he had traveled extensively and had a definite idea of the meaning of the imperial crown. He had been deeply impressed by his visit to India in 1905–06, and one of his first royal decisions was to return to India for a coronation durbar. The king believed his visit would "tend to allay unrest and, I am sorry to say, seditious spirit, which unfortunately exist in some parts of India." The cabinet approved the plan, and it was formally announced in England and India on March 23, 1911:

> ... WHEREAS it is OUR wish and desire OUR-SELVES to make known to all OUR loving subjects within OUR Indian Dominions that the said Solemnity [George's coronation] has been so celebrated, and to call to OUR Presence OUR Governors, Lieutenant-Governors, and other of OUR Officers, the Princes, Chiefs, and Nobles of the Native States under OUR Protection, and the Representatives of all the Provinces of OUR Indian Empire;
>
> Now WE do, by this OUR Royal Proclamation, declare OUR Royal intention to hold at Delhi on the twelfth day of December, one thousand nine hundred and eleven, an Imperial Durbar for the purpose of making known the said Solemnity of OUR Coronation: and WE do hereby charge and command OUR Right trusty and well-beloved Counsellor Charles, Baron Hardinge of Penshurst, OUR Viceroy and Governor-General of India, to take all necessary measures in that behalf....
>
> *God save the King-Emperor.*

King George had originally intended to crown himself at Delhi. Traditionally, kings are crowned by prelates, but emperors are kings of kings and crown themselves. It was pointed out, however, that this would set an unfortunate precedent. King George was emperor of India by law; therefore, no Indian coronation was required. If George was crowned separately in India, it would confuse the constitutional issue; and conceivably, each succeeding monarch of England might have to journey to Delhi to be crowned before being accepted as the legitimate ruler.

Moreover, since the king was emperor of India only by virtue of being king of England, a second coronation would necessitate a full-dress Church of England consecration service presided over by the archbishop of Canterbury (or so said the archbishop). Since it would be foolish to perform a Christian church service in Hindu-Moslem India —hardly the way to bring the king's Indian subjects closer to him—the whole idea was dropped.

But something was needed, and a compromise was reached: instead of crowning himself emperor, the king would appear, surrounded by imperial pomp and pageantry, and announce that he was already emperor by virtue of his coronation in England. The king would, moreover, appear at the durbar wearing the crown.

But which crown? The crown of India is the crown of England, but absolutely no one, not even the king, is allowed to take the crown out of the realm. A new crown would have to be made, and the question arose as to who should pay for it. The king was unwilling to pay for it himself; in any case, that would hardly have been seemly. It was still less appropriate for the money to come from the British treasury. Another suggestion, that it be paid for out of subscriptions raised in British India, was immediately vetoed on the grounds that it would be undignified for the king "to send round to collect money" for his own crown, and that it would be a catastrophe if the subscription failed to raise the required amount. It was finally decided that the crown would be paid for out of Indian government revenue.

But what should be done with the crown after the durbar was over? The original idea was to leave it in India, but a physical symbol of Indian sovereignty was a dangerous thing to have lying around; should it be stolen, there might be a real crisis of legitimacy. So the decision was made: the king would take the crown with him to India, wear it there, and bring it back to England to be placed in the Tower of London.

The king and queen left Buckingham Palace on the morning of November 11, 1911. They rode in an open landau through the streets of London to Victoria Station, where a "brilliant throng of the highest in the land" was present to see them off. At Portsmouth they boarded the newest and finest ship of the P&O, the H.M.S. *Medina*, which had been taken over by the Admiralty as a royal yacht.

After ceremonial visits at Gibraltar, Port Said, and Aden, the *Medina* arrived in Bombay on December 2 at the head of a squadron of four enormous cruisers. All the ships in the harbor flew a full complement of flags; the emperor's ship, in token of His Majesty's presence on board, carried the Admiralty flag at the fore, the royal standard at the main, and the Union Jack at the mizzen.

When the *Medina* dropped anchor, an imperial salute of 101 guns was fired; there would be many more of them over the next month. The governor-general came on board, as did other dignitaries of high estate. There was much saluting and piping, and many uniforms and flags and bands and helmet plumes.

Their Majesties left the *Medina* in the royal launch, while the guns of the harbor presented yet another imperial salute. The launch passed through a line of Bombay patrol boats, which saluted with raised oars, and finally it reached the pier. The emperor, wearing the white uniform of an admiral of the fleet, the ribbon of the Star of India, and the stars of the Orders of the Garter and the Indian Empire, ascended the steps and was greeted by the governor-general in the white dress uniform (and helmet plumes) of the Indian political service. This took place in the so-called Gateway to India, a giant pavilion constructed for the occasion with a high dome and golden minarets and an archway modeled after the ones used by the conquering kings of Assyria. After the greeting, the emperor proceeded to the throne pavilion along a red carpet—past lines of British and Indian troops in full dress, between rows of white columns each surmounted by a golden lion, and past a huge flagstaff with the royal standard. Attendants carried the red-and-gold *chatr* (imperial state umbrella) and the *suraj-mukhi* (imperial fan bearing the face of the sun), signaling the progress of the sovereign among all the white uniforms.

The throne pavilion was white and gold, with a canopy of royal blue silk. The thrones, of gilded teakwood nine feet high bearing the royal arms, the imperial crown, the Star of India, the lion and the unicorn, and other emblems of royal and imperial state, faced an amphitheatre seating three thousand people. Everywhere there were soldiers and people and flowers, silks and flags and colors of every description. A loyal address was offered, and presented in an elaborate silver casket. The emperor made his response. Then carriages were brought up, and the state progress through Bombay began. Three days of festivities followed, and finally, on December 5, the emperor boarded a train for Delhi.

The state entry into Delhi was intended to be a spectacular show, and it was. On the morning of December 7 the imperial train arrived in Salimgarh, an ancient fortress incorporated into the palace of Shah Jahan. The emperor stepped off, the royal standard rose above the Delhi gate of the fort, and the guns began another 101-gun imperial salute: first, 34 guns, then a *feu de joie* fired in sequence by the troops lining each side of the five-mile procession route to the imperial pavilion, then 33 more guns and another ten-mile *feu de joie*, and finally 34 more guns, another *feu de joie*, and the national anthem. The emperor had arrived.

A colorful pavilion with golden chairs of state had been erected below the red walls of Shah Jahan's palace. On the six-hundred-foot-long platform were the governor-general and other dignitaries in full uniform; the steps were lined by lancers, members of the Company of Gentlemen at Arms and the Royal Company of Archers, whom His Imperial Majesty had especially requested to be present. There were more soldiers, detachments from dozens of British and Indian units, and then two heralds in tabards bearing the royal coat of arms, one British (with a golden scepter) and one Indian (with a gold and ebony baton). They were seated on white horses, as were twenty-four trumpeters, dressed in cloth of gold, with banderoles of the royal arms on their silver trumpets (the drummer was on a black horse, with his white and gold drums carried on either side).

King George and Queen Mary accept the adulation of the masses at a huge garden party in Shah Jahan's palace in Delhi's Red Fort.

INDIA OFFICE LIBRARY AND RECORDS

The British trumpeters wore silver helmets; the Indians wore puggrees of pure gold.

The ruling princes and officials of the empire were received formally by the emperor and empress. Then on to another great pavilion where, on golden thrones surrounded by *chatrs, suraj-mukhis, morchals* (gold-encased peacock feathers), and *chanwars* (gold-handled yak tails), Their Majesties accepted the reverence of the massed rulers of India.

Time then for the state entry along a five-mile route lined with soldiers of every description in uniforms of every color. First there came the governors of the eight provinces of British India: the chief commissioner of the Central Provinces; the lieutenant-governors of the United Provinces, of Eastern Bengal and Assam, of Burma, Bengal, and the Punjab; and the governors of Madras and Bombay. They were followed by army units and high-ranking officers of His Imperial Majesty's Indian army. Then came heralds and state trumpeters, more army units, the military household of the emperor (including two maharajahs and one nawab), the governor-general's bodyguard (the senior unit of the Indian army, formed for Lord Hastings in 1777), the household cavalry, Life Guards, and Horse Guards, the commander in chief, the duke of Teck, and the personal staff of the emperor.

But where was the emperor? He *was*

Illustrated London News, January 25, 1936

An exotically garbed chief of Burma makes his obeisance before the emperor and empress. Virtually every prince, potentate, and nawab of India—including the eight splendidly arrayed rulers below—appeared at the ceremony and did homage to the British monarchs.

there, of course, in the uniform of a field marshal, but no one saw him. The empress, with her coach-and-six, her postilions and two state umbrellas and *suraj-mukhi*, was visible and obvious. But the emperor went unnoticed, and the crowd decided he wasn't there. He should, of course, have ridden an elephant. Lord Curzon had ridden one at the durbar of 1903; the Moguls had ridden elephants; and an Indian state elephant, painted and gilded and wearing a caparison of velvet and pearls and bearing an opulent howdah surmounted by a red-and-gold umbrella, is not likely to be overlooked. But the emperor had refused to ride an elephant because he wanted to be as close as possible to the people. He achieved that goal so successfully that he was mistaken for just

another general, and the dramatic center of the procession fell a bit flat.

Not all was lost, however, since there was much more of the procession to be seen. After the empress and more coaches, and the Imperial Cadet Corps and more army units, came the princes and feudatories.

Every ruling prince of the Indian Empire was present (except those attending the emperor and the nawab of Tonk, who was sick). There were 161 of them in all—each with his *chanwars* and *morchals* and flabella and mace bearers and bodyguards in chain-and-mail armor and riflemen with their ancient matchlocks and state swords and state umbrellas and drums and trumpets and battle axes and banners and every other symbol of power and sovereignty that hundreds of years of Asian history had devised.

The maharajah of Patiala, for example, was preceded by ten horses caparisoned in gold and silver. Then came halberdiers with *suraj-mukhis, chobdars* with gold and silver batons, horse-borne drums warning of the approach of the maharajah, a banner of state presented to him by Queen Victoria, and finally, the maharajah in a gold and silver coach escorted by a detachment of the Patiala Imperial Service Lancers. The nawab of Bahawalpur brought camels. Shan chiefs brought a hundred retainers in Chinese costume bearing spears, umbrellas, dahs, and

MAHARANA OF UDAIPUR

SULTAN OF LAHEJ

MAHARAJAH OF ALWAR

MAHARAJAH OF ORCHHA

ceremonial weapons. The maharajah of Orchha had a gold and silver palanquin and bearers carrying water from the Ganges. The rajah of Chamba had a detachment of Gaddi, local shepherd tribesmen playing native instruments. The maharajah of Sikkim brought warriors whose hair was braided about their waists. The sawbwa of Hsipaw wore a gold hat shaped like a pagoda. The maharajah of Travancore wore a robe of purple velvet edged with gold and a jeweled turban with bird-of-paradise plumes. And so it went, for 161 rulers and their retinues—all of them riding in the train of the emperor of India.

The emperor arrived at the imperial pavilion preceded by the customary artillery salvos, fanfares from the silver trumpets of the state trumpeters, and, at the moment of his actual arrival, the national anthem. The vice president of the legislative council approached the dais between two imperial mace bearers and presented an obsequious address of welcome. The emperor responded with a statement of his own. There were cheers, more fanfares, the national anthem again, and then the emperor descended to his camp.

The imperial encampment was a gigantic complex, a tent city that housed a quarter of a million people, not only in safety but in many cases splendor. It covered forty-five square miles, more than twice the area of Manhattan.

There were 475 separate camps—the emperor's camp alone covered 72 acres, had more than two thousand tents within its boundaries, and housed 2,140 people. The size of the other camps depended on the rank of the chief involved; those of the native princes were limited to 10,000 to 25,000 square yards each and housed from 100 to 500 attendants. Military camps varied according to the size of the detachments billeted there, but they too were substantial. In addition there were the camps of the provincial governors, camps for the governor-general and other dignitaries, and camps for the police, the Foreign Office, and the massed bands. There were stables, a central post office, railways, a market—everything necessary to support an instant imperial capital of 250,000 people.

A few statistics will illustrate the extent and complexity of the encampment. Forty-four miles of railway line were constructed, as well as a freight yard, 64 level crossings, 14 bridges, 29 fully equipped railway stations, 29 miles of siding, 10 miles of narrow-gauge railway with 19 small stations. Within four days 190 special trains and 256 regular trains converged on the imperial encampment; 75,000,000 pounds of goods and 100,000 parcels were delivered.

There were also 2,832 miles of telephone line and 1,000 miles of telegraph line; a main post office with 25 substations in which 700 people handled 5,250,000 pieces of mail; six major hospitals and a dispensary, and a veterinary hospital for the thousands and thousands of animals. There were 52 miles of water mains and 65 miles of distribution pipes to provide three million gallons of water a day for people, and half a million gallons an *hour* for the animals. A dairy with 2,000 milch cows and 500 workers produced 550,000 pounds of milk, 60,000 pounds of butter, and 12,000 pounds of cream during the nine-day stay. Animals in the encampment consumed almost two billion pounds of fodder. There was a market subject to rigid sanitary regulations, established in an attempt to control both contamination and prices, and native bazaars in every camp. And so on and so on. With or without the elephant, no one could fault the imperial style of George's encampment.

Their Majesties arrived at the camp on December 7, 1911, five days before the durbar. The intervening time was fully occupied. Each of the ruling chiefs was received by the emperor in the throne room of his pavilion. Those chiefs entitled to a return visit were visited by the governor-general. The empress received the ladies of high estate, and was presented, in true imperial fashion, with jewels. There was a state church service, an elaborate presentation of colors, a polo tournament, and much entertaining and dining and receiving.

The durbar itself, on Tuesday, December 12, 1911, was held in a gigantic amphitheatre. Public stands formed a vast semicircle in front and stands for the princes and notables formed a smaller semicircle behind. A series of narrowing platforms stood in the center of this vast area. The first was an octagonal platform 200 feet across. The second platform was of marble 81 feet square and 7 feet high, decorated with lotuses, a balustrade, and a turret at each corner. The third was also of white marble, and

RAO RAJAH OF BUNDI

NAWAB OF BAHAWALPUR

MAHARAJAH OF BIKANER

BEGUM OF BHOPAL

the fourth, 21 feet square, was covered with cloth of gold. Above that was the fifth platform, 8 feet square and a full 15 feet above the ground. On a golden carpet sat the two gilded imperial thrones. Suspended over the thrones was a rich red-and-gold canopy; the roof of the pavilion was bordered with crimson and gold velvet and bore five domes, all of gold. A causeway connected this pavilion to a much lower one, the homage pavilion.

The public stands were packed with thousands of people dressed in all manner of styles and colors. The stands of the princes and notables were also full: the first row was reserved for chiefs rating salutes of fifteen guns and more, the second row for those rating fewer than fifteen guns, and the third row for those chieftains who rated no guns at all. Everywhere there were soldiers, approximately fifty thousand in all, and massed bands of more than sixteen hundred musicians.

The veterans entered and marched to their assigned seats to the strains of "See, the Conquering Hero Comes." Then everyone rose, and the band played "Auld Lang Syne." A bugler announced the entry of the governor-general's procession. The band played the march from *Scipio*. Twenty minutes passed, and then the vanguard of the imperial procession appeared. Army units were first, as always, and then the governor-general's bodyguard, members of the household cavalry, and the imperial carriage, drawn by four bay horses. The emperor and empress wore their purple, gold, and ermine imperial robes of state (the emperor's robe was eighteen feet long). The emperor wore his crown, set with enormous sapphires, rubies, emeralds, and hundreds of sparkling diamonds. More military units followed.

When the imperial carriage entered the amphitheatre, a 101-gun salute began. The carriage proceeded slowly along one side of the public stands. As it passed, the troops presented arms and lowered their colors to the dust. At the foot of the homage pavilion, the emperor and empress descended from the carriage. The members of the household cavalry took up their positions on the outer sides of the homage pavilion, where the governor-general waited at the foot of the steps.

As the emperor and empress finally mounted the steps, the royal standard was unfurled, the troops presented arms, and the national anthem was played. The emperor and empress ascended the steps, turned, bowed to the assembled company, and sat down on their golden chairs of state. The pages of honor, in varied coats of white and gold adorned with diamond badges and jeweled daggers, arranged themselves gracefully on the steps. Disposed in various positions behind them were the royal entourage and the symbols of George's imperial dominion. The emperor commanded the master of ceremonies to open the durbar. There were flourishes and drum rolls, and then the emperor and empress rose from their seats. The one hundred thousand people present rose, too, and the emperor began to speak in a high, clear voice:

It is with genuine feelings of thankfulness and satisfaction that I stand here today among you. . . . It is a sincere pleasure and gratification to myself and the Queen-Empress to behold this vast assemblage and in it my Governors and trusty officials, my great Princes, the representatives of the peoples, and deputations from the military forces of my Indian dominions. I shall receive in person with heartfelt satisfaction the homage and allegiance which they loyally desire to render. I am deeply impressed with the thought that a spirit of sympathy and affectionate goodwill unites Princes and people with me on this historic occasion. . . . To all present, feudatories and subjects, I tender our loving greeting.

The emperor and empress then resumed their seats, and the homage began. First the governor-general approached the throne and kissed the emperor's hand. Then came the executive council, the ruling princes, the judiciary of Bengal, in robes and wigs, the legislative council of India, and the governors of each of the eight divisions of British India, attended by members of their councils, their judiciaries, and ruling princes of their areas.

Homage was done in various forms according to custom. The maharajah Holkar of Indore, for example, simply bowed, but the maharajah of Jaipur laid his sword on the steps of the throne and salaamed to the emperor and empress in turn. The maharajah of Panna kept his sword in his left hand, but salaamed with his right; the nawab of Janjira did the same, but did it three times. And so it went for forty-five minutes, while the 335 representatives of the peoples of India made obeisance to the sovereignty of the emperor and his consort and the band played suitably stately marches from European operas.

When it was over, the emperor and

A panoramic view of the encampment at Delhi: "The spectacle presented at night by the camp area . . . was remarkable and very beauti

empress rose and walked hand in hand around the base of the throne platform. They ascended the twenty-six steps to the summit and stood there for a moment before their golden thrones. They were now in the center of the amphitheatre, fifteen feet in the air, silhouetted against the Indian sky. It was a highly charged moment, and one whose significance could hardly be misunderstood. Then they were seated, and the trumpeters of the massed bands issued a trumpet blast to summon the heralds. The heralds entered on white horses. At the command of the emperor, the Delhi herald stood in his stirrups and read, from the satin scroll printed in gold, a proclamation assuring George's Indian subjects of "the deep affection with which WE regard OUR Indian Empire, the welfare and prosperity of which are and ever will be OUR constant concern." The assistant herald then read the same proclamation in Urdu. More trumpet fanfare. The national anthem was played by the sixteen hundred musicians in the massed bands. A hundred thousand people rose; fifty thousand troops presented arms. Thirty-four salvos of artillery from the north, a ten-mile *feu de joie*, six bars of the national anthem, 33 more salvos from the west, another *feu de joie*, six more bars of the national anthem, 34 more salvos from the east, another *feu de joie*, and the whole anthem once more.

Then more trumpet flourishes, and the Delhi herald called for three cheers for the emperor. Cheers were given. The assistant Delhi herald called for three cheers for the empress. Cheers were given. Their Majesties returned to the homage pavilion. More fanfares. Exit

heralds. End of durbar . . . almost. The emperor rose again and spoke:

We are pleased to announce to our people that . . . We have decided upon the transfer of the Seat of the Government of India from Calcutta to the ancient Capital of Delhi, and simultaneously, and as a consequence of that transfer, the creation at as early a date as possible of a Governorship for the Presidency of Bengal, of a new Lieutenant-Governorship in Council administering the areas of Behar, Chota Nagpur and Orissa, and of a Chief Commissionership of Assam, with such administrative changes and redistribution of boundaries as our Governor-General in Council, with the approval of our Secretary of State for India in Council, may in due course determine.

These announcements were quite unexpected. The moving of the capital had an important impact on the politics and society of India—of Calcutta society in particular—and required that a new city be built at Delhi. The new administrative divisions reversed the unpopular partition of Bengal made by Lord Curzon. It was a highly dramatic moment.

With that, the master of ceremonies was commanded to close the durbar. Everyone rose again. The national anthem was played, and the procession descended from the pavilion. It proceeded around the other side of the semicircle of the public stands and out of the amphitheatre in precisely symmetrical fashion. Exit the emperor, exit the governor-general, exit the notables.

Then the people poured down from the stands and did the nonviolent Indian equivalent of tearing up the goal posts. They prostrated themselves before the thrones and rubbed their heads with the

earth the emperor had trod upon; they reached up to touch the fringes of the carpets on which the emperor had stood. And then one hundred thousand people passed silently before the empty throne of the emperor of India.

And that was the coronation durbar of 1911. It is difficult to evaluate its effects. In historical terms, they were small. There was some increase in loyalty to the raj and some diminution of "unrest and sedition"; those who knew him said the effect on King George himself was profound. But he is gone now, and so is the raj.

The most important thing about the durbar is that we remember it. If there was a high noon of empire, it was December 12, 1911. In a few years that high sun would be eclipsed by World War I, and from then on nothing would be the same. There would be only two more emperors of India: one was not even crowned, and the second was deposed after yet another war. The overseas empire has been reduced to a mixed and miscellaneous collection of islands and a great many glorious and misunderstood memories. England itself is in desperate straits, and glorious memories do not serve to heat the house or feed the children. But to those who take pleasure in the details of great ceremonies, who are amazed by the trappings of personal sovereignty, and who care about the history of the British Empire, the durbar of 1911 has a certain old snapshot, bittersweet quality. It was the best of all possible durbars and it was the last.

David F. Phillips currently teaches in Taiwan. This article was adapted from a longer, unpublished work on the durbar.

twinkling lines of myriad lights stretching far in all directions, and producing the effect of some enormous pattern arranged on a symmetric scheme."

Awash on a Sea of Vodka

Upon it sails the Soviet ship of state—a very tight ship indeed

By ISRAEL SHENKER

CHAS B SLACKMAN

Prince Vladimir of Kiev is said to have made Russia Christian rather than Moslem because, as he put it, "It is impossible to be happy in Russia without strong drink."

What was bad enough for princes and czars is bad enough for commissars: drink was a plague then and drink is a plague today, moonshiners flourished then and they thrive today. The czars grew wealthy on vodka revenue, and today the Soviet regime depends heavily on those taxes.

Vodka's first entrepreneur was Ivan the Terrible. In the sixteenth century he set up what became known as Czar's Bars, and the practice of enticing the peasantry to drink not only to the czar but for his profit was well-launched. To preserve his monopoly, Ivan had moonshiners beaten with the knout or tossed into the river. During the next century, people selling spirits illegally had a bottle of their merchandise tied to their neck and were whipped through the streets, though culprits were eventu-

ally allowed to stand in place, barefoot, and were then simply beaten on the legs.

Though profitable to the czarist regime, drunkenness became an open scandal. Then a church patriarch persuaded Czar Alexis I (1645–1676) to forbid the sale of more than one glass of spirits to anyone. At the same time, the czar ordered that his alcohol revenues had to rise every year. To ensure the good faith of barkeepers, they were required to kiss the cross as they took the oath of office, and the name for a saloonkeeper became the opprobrious "one who kisses." In 1676, however, the fourteen-year-old Czar Feodor III banned saloons from his realm. In view of his tender years, he was forgiven his excess of virtue, and the measure was quickly undone.

It was Peter the Great (1682–1725) who elevated drunkenness to its heights. He instituted the Imperial Conclave of Drunkards, which met periodically to relive the memories of blasphemies past. Its charter required members to drink

daily until drunk and never to go to bed sober. When suitably oiled, the conclave would ride in public procession in sleighs drawn by bears or goats, or by four pigs in harness.

Later czars and czarinas vacillated on details of spiritous policy. Sometimes they encouraged bidding for retail rights, and at other times tried a system of outright government monopoly. By about 1860, 40 per cent of government revenue came from spirits, and those licensed to sell alcohol gave regular payoffs (called "sinless revenues") to corrupt officials.

In 1863, the enlightened government that liberated the serfs decided that free people who had cheap spirits of good quality would drink with moderation. So the price of vodka was cut by about two-thirds; sales increased 215 per cent in one year. To inhibit prolonged libation, the ingenious regime forbade saloons to have furniture. No less ingenious judges joined the crusade against excesses: they levied fines, which were paid in vodka and drunk on the spot by the judges and the parties to the suit.

Serf or free, the average man had little time for imbibing during the workaday week, but with fifty-two Sundays and no end of saints' days and other holidays, there were endless opportunities for drunkenness. So the government made yet another effort to combine the pleasures of revenue with the demands of temperance. In 1894 Count Sergei Witte, the minister of finance, launched a fundamental reform: a monopoly law providing strict government supervision of distillation and sale. It worked unprecedentedly well, and the czar's government began accumulating huge surpluses of cash and drunkards. By 1912 there were 2,983 legal distilleries and 26,016 legal retail establishments.

The tide of temperance lapped at this fortune. By the reform of 1894 moderate subsidies were allocated to temperance organizations, but the groups were evidently busy with other things. The Lublin chapter, for example, had 776 members—6 of them active. Nevertheless, the alcohol monopoly officials grew

62

intemperate whenever temperance propagandists showed zeal. When doctors at a medical congress in 1904 discussed the drink monopoly, several of the most outspoken critics paid for their exuberance by being exiled to Siberia.

Not too long afterward, a czarist imperial councilor announced to an international congress in Milan that there was one drunkard to 16,962 Parisians, one to 1,020 Viennese, and one to 25 citizens of St. Petersburg. Even Russian schoolchildren drank vodka: of the boys aged eight to thirteen in Moscow schools, 66 per cent imbibed.

The Duma earnestly discussed alcohol's depredations in 1907, 1908, 1911, and 1912. It finally acted, reducing the alcohol content in vodka from 40 per cent to 37 per cent. But Duma-member Michael Tschelishev indignantly declared that "Russian bureaucracy does not want the people to become sober, for it is easier autocratically to rule a drunken mob than a sober people." He proposed a bill requiring every vodka bottle to be labeled "poison." Tolstoy designed a sample label. The Duma triumphantly passed the bill. The imperial council killed it.

Came World War I, and to save grain and morale, the czar instituted prohibition. It was the signal some were waiting for, and the Moscow city council wired that it "lays before the feet of Your Imperial Majesty feelings of exquisite joy." In the first six months of exquisite prohibition, the ministry of finance turned up 2,825 moonshine stills. It also discovered that without taxes on alcohol there were no longer surpluses of anything except red ink. Between 1900 and 1913, 25 to 30 per cent of all state revenue had come from alcohol, a staggering total that was hard for John Gunther to swallow when he wrote *Inside Russia Today*. He consigned the intelligence to a footnote, writing: "I have read . . . but cannot quite believe it."

By the testimony of his eyes, Gunther wrote of post-czarist citizenry: "Russian drunks are among the most vivid, sodden and uncompromising drunks ever known anywhere." The Revolution was

supposed to change all that, produce a new society, a new and nobler man. In 1923 weak vodka was authorized, and then strong vodka. The government plunged back into the vodka business, in time to whet the thirst of the poet Sergei Esenin: "Oh, today's a great day for the Russian/the moonshine vodka's flowing/and the noseless accordionist's singing/of the Volga and the secret police."

In 1925 Stalin declared that it was better "to get revenue from vodka than to go hat in hand to foreign capitalists." Two years later he said that banning vodka would simply encourage peasants to produce their own. That same year, the Five-Year Plan called for a 31 per cent decline in vodka sales. Nonetheless, vodka production rose 30 per cent.

In 1958 Khrushchev tried to discourage drinking by increasing the prices of all alcoholic drinks except beer by 21 per cent. Drinking dropped only 5.4 per cent, but statistics showed that families spent less on food. Khrushchev also restored the ban on serving anyone more than one glass of spirits. When it was suggested this would simply encourage bar-hopping, Khrushchev replied that the drinker would at least sober up between hops.

"When I drink a glass of vodka," as the old saw has it, "I'm another man, and the other man needs a glass of vodka." D.T.'s are "white fever" in Russia; what Americans call pink elephants is a singular "green snake." In Latvia one winter, so many of the men employed as Father Frost (Santa Claus)

had taken so much vodka as antifreeze that the thaw was almost beyond the descriptive powers of editorialists. In fact, Soviet tipplers will go to almost any lengths to protect their drinking rights. One group of farm officials even shot down a crop-dusting plane that was disturbing their picnic.

All this would be cheer enough were it not for the added complication of moonshine: the Soviet Union ranks first in the world in consumption of distilled spirits, and moonshine makes up more than a quarter of that alcohol.

Russians call moonshine *samogon*, from the words *sam* (self) and *gnat* (to chase, to distill). Most *samogon* is produced by small, family-run stills, usually in rural areas, but production is so widespread—one economist puts the estimate at a billion liters a year—that the supreme court once felt obliged to issue special directives for enforcement of anti-*samogon* laws.

But détente—the relaxation of tensions—has its reasons that the law ignores. The population has few escape mechanisms, and it will risk fines and imprisonment for the sake of the release that *samogon* provides. Professor Vladimir G. Treml of Duke University estimates that consumption of spirits in the Soviet Union has been rising over 5 per cent per annum per person of drinking age (fifteen and over). In 1913 taxes on spirits were about 5.4 per cent of the national income, and recently the figure has been about 5.9 per cent. The government's income from alcohol is more than enough to cover the official amount budgeted for defense.

Of course, there is a secret defense budget as well, but the government collects no taxes toward it from *samogon*. Who knows what glorious new guns, and rockets to the moon, the U.S.S.R. could afford if it could only draw profits—as well as alcohol and consolation—from *samogon*.

Though Israel Shenker's last name means "saloonkeeper," he has never touched vodka—not even during his two years as a Moscow correspondent for Time.

AN ARCHITECTURE OF GRANDEUR

The Beaux-Arts Tradition Reconsidered

Now that twentieth-century modernism is dead, the Museum of Modern Art allows itself a backward glance

"What style will the Opéra be?" the Empress Eugénie delicately inquired of its architect, Charles Garnier, the grandmaster of the nineteenth-century Beaux-Arts style. Would the new ornament of Paris in the imperial 1860's be Louis XIV? Louis XV? Louis XVI? *"C'est du Napoléon III,"* Garnier elegantly retorted. And so it was, for no building could have been more symbolic of the Second Empire: quilted with wealth and power, lush of surface, overwhelmingly ceremonious, ritually ordered. It symbolized something else, too: the Romantic tradition of design instilled in aspiring architects at the Ecole des Beaux-Arts, which, since the time of Napoleon I, had been the arbiter of taste in all French buildings.

The Opéra, that conjunction of classical Rome with the flamboyant Baroque of the seventeenth century, was fated to become an architectural bugbear within forty years of its completion. Except for the monument to Victor Emmanuel II in Rome, no nineteenth-century building has borne more ritual execration from modern architectural students and their teachers. To glance at it was to be contaminated; one might turn, like Lot's disobedient wife,

In an atelier, architecture students from the Ecole des Beaux-Arts work at drawingboards. One Beaux-Arts alumnus, J.L.C. Garnier, drew the scheme, opposite, for the staircase of the Paris Opéra.

into a column of ormolu. So I felt properly sinful when, as an architecture student fresh from Australia on my first night in Paris, I crept, ticket in hand, through Garnier's wicked and wasteful entrance portico. Then, as I wandered through the foyers and up the Grand Staircase, like a minnow inside the rippling esophagus of a whale, I realized that for the first time in my life I was being worked over by a building. No matter how one might disapprove of its bombastic exuberance, those profuse surfaces of malachite, serpentine, plush, and ormolu, it worked. One walked dif-

ferently. One's breathing expanded to match the architecture. There was a sense of secular procession, of rituals dedicated to pleasure. If this was pomp, could it be so very bad? A strutting, preening public architecture, certainly; but how well matched to its purpose as an opera house; how rhythmic, how artificial, how rich in content and captivating in its illusions! Months later, back in class in Australia, I tried to explain this heretical enjoyment to our design lecturer. He listened glumly, and at the end of my hesitant outpourings he remarked that for the price of two tickets to the Opéra I could have caught a bus to Poissy and looked at what was left of Le Corbusier's Villa Savoye. "Why did you want to look at Garnier's junk?" he demanded.

That was in 1959. Now, seventeen years later, a revisionist spirit has entered the appraisal of nineteenth-century art and architecture. A new curiosity about the "official" culture of the nineteenth century has set in. It is no longer necessary to strike partisan attitudes about the aesthetic issues of 1875; they are archaeology, and interesting as such. Even William Bouguereau, that nineteenth-century Salon painter of glossy

By ROBERT HUGHES

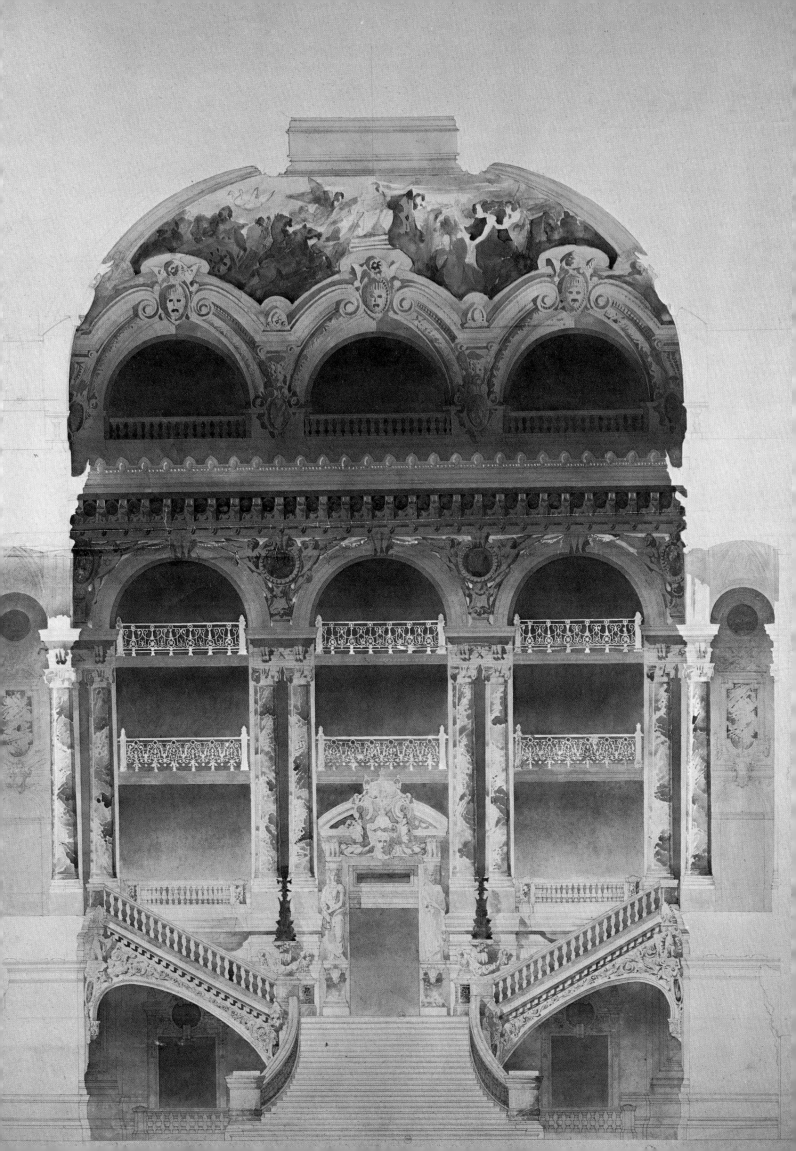

nudes, has had a retrospective in New York. Last fall the Museum of Modern Art, arbiter of contemporary taste, joined the revisionists with an exhibition that ten years ago would have seemed a betrayal of its modernist goals. It is a collection of some two hundred designs and presentation drawings by students at the Ecole des Beaux-Arts during the nineteenth century, Garnier among them.

For decades all these elaborate drawings lay uncatalogued in the attic of the Ecole on the Left Bank, across the Seine from the Louvre. They have been brought to light by the Museum of Modern Art's curator of architecture, Arthur Drexler, who has prepared a catalogue that includes a full battery of scholarly essays by architectural historians David Van Zanten, Richard Chafee, and Neil Levine. It is the kind of excavation job that can only happen at the end of a period; since the dominant image of modern architecture, the International Style, is now played out, the time has come to look at its traditional enemy. It turns out, amazingly enough, that in some ways the two schools of architecture are not so very different.

History is written by the victors. This helps explain the violence with which twentieth-century architectural critics assailed Beaux-Arts training and design. The aim was to annihilate it, to make it impossible ever to look with respect at such work again; in the process, much of French architecture produced between 1820 and 1900 was written off. Siegfried Giedion, hardly a sympathetic critic, wrote that nineteenth-century architects, "in order to compensate for their own lack of expressive force, had misused eternal names by pilfering from history. . . . This was the period of pseudomonumentality." Indeed, some Beaux-Arts architecture was so "bad" that it did not exist as style. "The nineteenth century," pronounced a German architectural historian, Jurgen Joedlicke, in 1959, "developed no characteristic art forms in spatial composition

The Paris Opéra, Garnier's masterpiece, opened in 1875. With its arcaded entrance, neo-Baroque façade, and oversize statuary, it makes an impressive setting for grand opera — and for operagoers.

J. L. C. GARNIER

and planning. It was an epoch without a building style of its own." The Beaux-Arts building, according to the party line, was cold and pompous *patisserie*, florid in detail, inhumanly symmetrical in plan, indifferent to function or material, blind to the technological spirit of its age. Unlike the work of nineteenth-century engineers such as Joseph Paxton, Henry de Dion, and Gustave Eiffel, the Beaux-Arts style permitted nothing to be developed from it. It could only be buried in ridicule, and that is precisely what was done: by 1950, the very idea that any Beaux-Arts building might be worth looking at, or that studying its design might bring a clearer understanding of the nineteenth century, had been lost.

No doubt the moral opprobrium heaped on the Beaux-Arts was made easier by the fact that twentieth-century dictators admired it. Stalin's official architecture was a debased parody of Beaux-Arts blocks and colonnades. The same was true of Albert Speer's work for Hitler—who himself loved the Paris Opéra: it was the first building he visited on his triumphant entry into Paris in

June, 1940. It was lit up, as for a gala performance, at six in the morning and Hitler was driven straight to it. He had long treasured a set of reproductions of Garnier's drawings, and now he went striding up the Grand Staircase and strutting through the foyer, completely at home, immersed in grandeur. The lesson to democrats is plain: you can tell a building by the company it keeps.

In any case, the clients of the successful Beaux-Arts architects—the merchant bankers and bureaucrats of the Second Empire, the upper part of the social pyramid that terminated in the figure of Louis Napoleon—had long been standard targets of modernist rhetoric. The underdog artist's contempt for Beaux-Arts extravagance, for example, goes back to Baudelaire's sardonic description, in *Les Yeux des Pauvres* (1864), of a luxurious new café:

The very gaslight was flaring with the ardour of a neophyte . . . on the dazzling white of the walls, on the brilliantly polished sheet-glass mirrors, on the gilt of the mouldings and the cornices, on the friezes showing chubby-faced pages holding hounds that strained at the leash . . . on nymphs and goddesses bearing baskets on their heads piled high with pastries, fruits and game, while Hebes and Ganymedes held out at arm's length little pitchers of Bavarian cream or multicolored sticks of Bavarian ice: all of history and all of mythology pressed into the service of gluttony.

In contrast to this class-bound opulence, modernist architecture was to be a democratic answer to social crisis, or so the fathers of the International Style believed. "The balance of society," Le Corbusier wrote in his manifesto of 1923, *Vers une Architecture*, "comes down to a question of building. We conclude with these justifiable alternatives: *Architecture or Revolution*." For us, the idea of modernity has lost the fervor it had for its pioneers. To them it meant a unique fusion of romance and rationality, and it sprang from the same roots as Marxism. Latent in technology and mass production were scarcely imaginable utopias. The machine had the power to transform society, and it was, moreover, aesthetically pleasing. The Italian futurist Filippo Marinetti thought a racing car at full throttle more beautiful than the Winged Victory of Samothrace, and Le Corbusier compared the design of a 1919 Farman passenger plane with that of the Parthenon. Technology meant precise function, a weeding out of the superfluous: in a word, planning. "You will inevitably arrive," Le Corbusier wrote, "at the 'House-tool,' the mass-production house, available for everyone, incomparably healthier than the old kind (and morally so too). . . . But it is essential to create the right state of mind for living in mass-production houses." People, no less than their shelters, needed replanning. Revise the shelter and one improves the people.

Walter Gropius and Mies van der Rohe in Germany, no less than Le Corbusier in France, believed in the vision of the architect as seer and sociological priest. Architecture could transform society. To match an ideal architecture of steel and glass, based on prefabrication and functional clarity, a new type of person would arise—Le Corbusier's modular figure, as it were, in flesh and blood: a lover of speed and socialism, plain food, fresh paint, hygiene, and sun baths.

But as our century wore on, it became apparent that the International Style was not going to change society. The glass curtain wall turned out to be just as much the expression of a ruling bureaucratic elite in the twentieth century as the malachite-and-gilt foyer in the nineteenth. By the mid-1950's, the machine-detailed thrust of a skyscraper block had become the symbol of corporate efficiency. Far from provoking a socialist millennium, Mies and Gropius had given American capitalism its house style. This fact was not lost on other architects. As Gio Ponti remarked in 1961, when his sleek headquarters for the Pi-

relli company was finally finished in Milan: "I grant, and I am pleased, that architecture (good architecture) should be a means of advertising, and I recommend it to all. . . . When I happen to meet people who are anxious to live on in History I never fail to advise them to invest in the 'Bank of Architecture' which will assure them of a 'security,' which is their name, of unfailing quotation."

Perhaps the most successful use of a building as advertisement in these boom years was the Seagram Building, completed in 1958. Nobody knows how many drinkers were converted to Seagram's whiskey by Mies van der Rohe's and Philip Johnson's design—probably not very many—but the payoff of grounding a corporate name in the history of modern architecture has been immense. With its immaculate bronze tartan grid and its fanatically elegant detailing, the Seagram Building was the Parthenon of the curtain wall. But it had hardly been brought to Park Avenue by leftist social theorists.

In their old age, the masters of Bauhaus internationalism—Gropius

HENRI LABROUSTE

For the arches, beams, and columns of the reading room of the Bibliothèque Nationale—France's treasure-house of books and manuscripts—Labrouste used cast iron, a popular material at the time.

and Mies—were regarded as refugees from fascism who had defended liberty against the crushing power of the State. Yet, as Charles Jencks points out in his brilliant study, *Modern Movements in Architecture*, the idea that they were repelled by Hitler is not completely true. Gropius designed buildings for the Nazis and "as late as June 1934 . . . wrote letters to Goebbels defending the 'Germanness' of the new architecture and calling it a synthesis 'of the classical and Gothic traditions.'" Mies van der Rohe accepted Hitler's commission to design a new Reichsbank for Berlin in 1933, and turned out a curtain wall of such crystalline severity—not to say blankness—as to prefigure a good deal of the corporate architecture in Manhattan today.

The point is not, of course, that International Style building is "fascist." Hitler did, after all, close the Bauhaus and ban modernism from Germany. But the International Style was based on absolute and abstract systems that tend to appeal to the authoritarian mind. Mies, in his late work of the 1960's, raised his passion for order to a point where the buildings became unworkable. His Gallery of the Twentieth Century in Berlin is one example: to preserve the integrity of Mies' favorite form, the gridded glass block, the works of art had to be relegated to the basement, where at least the walls could have pictures hung on them.

Still, Mies' buildings do have an historical eminence as a specimen of elegance that makes them tolerable. But no such excuse can be made for his more routine imitators. By the 1960's most of the glass skyscrapers going up in America had about the same relation to the "classics" of the International Style as the very worst Beaux-Arts wedding cakes had to the seventeenth-century Baroque palaces they imitated. The glass boxes were pastiche architecture, a routine ordering of cut-rate cells. Their blank walls were repetitive and threatening,

LE CORBUSIER

THE VILLA SAVOYE

FARMAN BIPLANE, 1919

Early in this century, as the Beaux-Arts tradition waned, architects began to take an iconoclastic interest in technology. Le Corbusier, for example, compared the functionalism of the Farman biplane, right, with the sublime lines of the Parthenon. The architect's Villa Savoye, built near Paris in 1929, and later destroyed, has a sparse, machine-age elegance that was foreign to Beaux-Arts taste.

drenched in images that were bureaucratic and authoritarian, except that, unlike the average nineteenth-century town hall, they were faceless. The International Style in its decrepitude was as aesthetically feeble and morally suspect as the Beaux-Arts had ever been. No wonder that the most admired American architect of recent years was, until his death in 1974, Louis Kahn, whose work was rooted in a Beaux-Arts sensibility.* The time is ripe to dig up the once hated Ecole, and inspect it with more calm.

Between 1819, when it rose from the wreck of the Royal Academies suppressed by the Revolution, and 1968, when the rebellious students of Paris forced its last collapse, the Ecole des Beaux-Arts dominated French architecture. It was *the* school; and though its power was dissipated in the twentieth century, in the nineteenth it was nearly absolute. If an architect could call himself an *ancien élève de l'Ecole des Beaux-Arts*, it counted for more, at least inside France, than a formal degree from any other design school in the world. This was partly snobbery: yet it was so prominent an institution that even the public took an interest in student competitions. In 1829, a brilliant young student, Henri Labrouste, sent back from Rome his required studies in archaeological reconstruction for the Ecole's judgment: twenty-three sheets of measured drawings of the massive Doric temples at Paestum. One academician, Quatremère

*See "Brick is Stingy . . ." Autumn, 1974

de Quincy, rebuked the young man for getting the measurements "wrong" (they were not), and the subsequent fight held the attention of the French press for weeks, becoming a symbol of the battle between youthful inquiry and entrenched conservatism. It is hard to imagine the *New York Times* so greeting a similar dispute at the Yale School of Architecture. There could not *be* such a dispute again, since reconstruction of the classical past is no longer an architect's basic training. Nevertheless, the Beaux-Arts curriculum was so influential that as late as 1957, as a first-year student in Australia, I spent eye-blurring weeks hunched over an obligatory rendering of the Parthenon, done in "not less than seventy-five" washes of Chinese ink. To appreciate the showy, obsessive virtuosity of a Parthenon reconstruction like Loviot's (page 72), it helps to have made one's

WALTER GROPIUS

In 1919, Walter Gropius founded the Bauhaus—an opposite pole to the Beaux-Arts school. Gropius and his associates taught their students to collaborate on industrial-age projects both large and small—from teacups to mass-produced housing, like the experiment in low-cost units at right.

own mess of those flutings and metopes.

In the modern sense of the word, the Ecole des Beaux-Arts was hardly a "school" at all. For most of the nineteenth century it gave no degrees. It did provide regular, although not compulsory, lectures in architectural history, construction, and theory, and it furnished its students with a library and an imposing jumble of grimy plaster casts, which they were expected to draw. The idea of requiring an architecture student to sketch a cast of the *Laocoon* seems absurd today, but it did not in the nineteenth century, when the decoration of buildings with cartouches and ornamental figures was still part of architecture.

Beaux-Arts professors were, at least in the eyes of their students, remote and silent figures, the embodiments of centralized law. When a student presented a project to one of them, he got his mark, and that was that. There was no question of a dialogue between them. The professor's role was less to teach than to judge. One learned the *practice* of architecture outside. In fact, one had to be apprenticed to a practicing architect before enrolling at the Ecole. The first step for an aspiring architect was to learn the techniques of drawing. He might even pay some hack artist for guidance in the simpler tricks.

Then the student had to find a patron, an established architect with a studio. The student paid his patron for instruction and regular advice on the projects set by the Ecole, and in return the architect would give him drawing-board

THE BAUHAUS

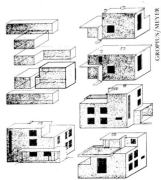

HOUSING, CIRCA 1922

space in a frigid, candle-lit office. Students chose their patrons, rather as the medieval scholars at the universities of Paris had selected their own professors. Sometimes students flocked to an architect because of the fire and originality of his ideas—the iconoclastic Labrouste, for instance, had a studio full of paying apprentices between 1830 and 1856. But most nineteenth-century architecture students had a firm sense of realpolitik and tended to study with the conservative, solid old buffers, who had a vote (or at least, friends) on the Beaux-Arts juries.

Sponsored by patrons, students entered the Ecole in the so-called second class and were given a set number of design problems to work out, involving either *esquisses* (rough sketches) or *projets rendus* (full renderings). They had to pass written examinations and submit drawings on the difficult problems of construction, and then, once they had enough credits—which might take years—they went on to the first class. Each year, the first-class students would compete for the most coveted of all architectural awards: the Grand Prix de Rome. The recipient won public acclaim as the most gifted student in France, and four or five years' study at the French Academy in Rome. Each year, the winner would send back to the Ecole his *envoi*, or consignment of drawings: a reconstruction of some ancient building, like the "Restoration of the Parthenon" executed by Loviot. And finally, fortified by a thorough understanding of antiquity, polished by the great finishing school of classicism south of the Alps, the Prix de Rome laureate would come back to France and, if he behaved himself, to a guaranteed income from the state for work on public buildings and, perhaps, a teaching career as head of his own atelier.

Not only was the Beaux-Arts course heavily slanted toward archaeological reconstruction. It was by modern standards curiously unrelated to the realities of actual construction. Projects were scaled to the student's experience: second-classers, or *nouveaux*, worked on

SEAGRAM BUILDING, 1958

Hitler commissioned Mies van der Rohe to design the Berlin Reichsbank in 1933. It was never built but its curtain wall reappears in the Seagram Building in New York. Mies's dictum that "less is more" eventually evolved into a spare simplicity that has often been honored by second-rate imitations, much as Beaux-Arts masterpieces had been aped by lesser talents.

MIES VAN DER ROHE

REICHSBANK, 1933

modest projects—a small villa, a post office, a provincial museum, or, for the colonies, such amenities as the "Fountain in a Roadside Oasis in Algeria" (page 71), by nineteen-year-old Gabriel Ancelet in 1848. Senior students would attack more grandiose buildings: a gigantic bourse, a vast granary, a railway terminal, or "The Principal Staircase of the Palace of a Sovereign" (pages 76–77), the prize-winning design of 1863.

The realities of building, starting with the peculiarities of the site, did not intrude in these vast and suavely conceived programs. There *was* no site; it was paper architecture inhabiting an ideal space. Yet an almost hallucinatory reality exists in the drawings because of the extraordinary quality of the rendering. One can safely say that no architect ever rendered like the student at the Ecole des Beaux-Arts in the nineteenth century. Who, today, could turn out a drawing, on a sheet of paper twenty feet wide, like Jean Camille Formigé's railway station (page 72), with its faience decorations and Assyrian livestock, every pop-rivet casting its own shadow? What renderer of condominiums and curtain walls could attempt Duquesne's elevation of "A Pilgrimage Church," an apparition of winding ramps culminating in a Brunelleschi dome, all of it materializing out of a blotchy, liquid gray wash? The scale of Beaux-Arts student designs seems megalomaniac; how could such projects, one wonders, equip a student for

design in the real world? Yet curiously enough, they did—after a fashion: for the students were being prepared for a "real world" of architecture very different from today's.

To us, the idea of architecture has the broadest meaning. It covers anything built, from a toolshed to a factory, from a cottage to a skyscraper. But to an educated Frenchman a century ago, *l'architecture* was more restricted and exalted. It meant the design of important public buildings: ministries, banks, museums, railroad stations, palaces. The heyday of the Ecole des Beaux-Arts was also, by no coincidence, the time of France's greatest colonial, industrial, and governmental expansion. Since 1800, what amounted to a new class—the bureaucracy—had been called into being. Before Napoleon, French bureaucrats were relatively few, their offices mere appendages to the actual seat of power, the throne. But with the arrival of the *Code Napoléon*, that vast and detailed edifice of law, the civil servants needed to run it multiplied. The number of state ministries shot up, as did their size. The bounds of France's empire would never be wider, but the drive toward centralization was intense. Paris, the navel of the civilized world, required an architecture of prosperous authority. The new buildings were symbols of the official ego, demonstrations of state power, but they were also intended as benevolent public display. They were designed for a self-confident bourgeoisie convinced, with reason, that it had inherited the earth.

These richly decorated official buildings are now said to be wasteful, but they fulfilled their purpose admirably: they confirmed what David Van Zanten calls the "bourgeois landscape" of urban France. Today, one could not build anything like the stately arcades with which Charles Percier, the first great figure of the Ecole des Beaux-Arts, transformed the rue de Rivoli. It would be impossible to try, simply because nobody knows how to cut stone or lay brick that well anymore. (One of the reasons Beaux-Arts design was discredited in America after 1900 was the difficulty of finding craftsmen who could give the buildings something better than machine-cut decoration.) But in France in the nineteenth century, the skills and the materials—iron, glass, bronze, brick, and the honey-colored limestone that now forms the tawny skin of Paris —were at hand. The creation of a sense of well-being was the legitimate business of building. The purpose of a public structure was, in Arthur Drexler's phrase, "to assure you that you are the reason for the republic."

Consider the contrast between the terminals of their age and ours: the nineteenth-century metropolitan railroad station, the airport of twentieth-century America. A passenger departing from the Gare de l'Est in the 1850's entered the arcaded porch that drew him toward the big central lunette, a secular cathedral window, behind which stretched the immense vault above the platforms. There was no "functional" reason for the high ceilings in the passenger concourse. Instead, they provided a ceremonial space, and the traveler was the subject of the ceremony. Wasteful though it would seem to a modern cost-accountant—all that carved limestone! —the architecture informed the traveler that he was important, a creature of substance and worth. No airport in the world does that. By contrast, the modern terminal, under its skin of brisk efficiency, manipulates the passenger: harried by the plan, he is reduced to a unit in a flow chart. The hard architecture, with discomforts built in to drive people into the concessions to spend their money, renders the traveler small and banal.

The best Beaux-Arts architecture was at pains to keep the sense of occasion alive, on all levels: planning, structure, symbolism, décor. If we only look at the structure, we are apt to miss its meaning. In general, being most interested in its own ancestry, the twentieth century only wanted to see one aspect of nineteenth-century architecture—engineering. It looked for protostructuralists in the Beaux-Arts, and found one in Henri Labrouste (1801–1875), who, between 1843 and 1850, designed the Bibliothèque Ste. Geneviève and the soaring ironed-framed domes of the Bibliothèque Nationale. The Bibliothèque Ste. Geneviève's reading room, with its slender iron columns carrying twin vaults on curved iron trusses, is an exquisitely refined use of exposed metal structure. But to call it, on that account, a "modern" building—a prediction of the International Style—is to misread it. Though Labrouste took issue with the teaching system at the Ecole des Beaux-Arts (none of his own students ever got the Prix de Rome), he was entirely at one with its culture—especially its insistence on elegant detailing and richness of imagery. In fact, the reading room of the Bibliothèque Ste. Geneviève can be seen as an organic metaphor—the equivalent of the branching, interlacing trees in the Luxembourg Gardens where students sat with their library books.

But the foundation of Beaux-Arts design, the regulator that controlled the sense of expansive spectacle in the best of the buildings, was the plan. As the architect A. F. Victor Laloux remarked to his students, "You can put forty good façades on a good plan, but without a good plan you cannot have a good façade." What a good plan boiled down to, in Beaux-Arts terms, was a series of stately axes punctuated by dramatic revelations of mass and space. It had to be logical and clear. "The public need never ask the way in a good plan," pronounced one professor, Julien Guadet, who nevertheless held that there were no clear-cut recipes for making one. Oddly enough, Beaux-Arts buildings have long been accused of being mechanical in plan—an axis there, a minor axis here, symmetries thus and so, as if done with a cooky cutter. In fact, the theorists and professors of the time tended to be almost coy in their reluctance to make prescriptions.

If one does not need to ask the way, it can only mean that the plan is intelligible. This harmony was summed up by the Beaux-Arts professors in the idea of *la marche*, literally "the walk." Instead of experiencing a building room by room, as one static unit after another, you did it by traveling continuously through it. The idea was linked to a favorite European social form that has never caught on in the United States— the *promenade* in France, the *passeggiata* in Italy. Beaux-Arts architects strove to put this swagger inside their buildings as well as out. Garnier, in particular, was explicit about it. In 1871, four years before the Opéra opened, he set forth his theory in his book *Le Théâtre*, in which every aspect of designing an opera house is analyzed in terms of ceremonial movement. (One did not go to the Opéra just to see a performance; one was also there, especially in the late nineteenth century, to enjoy the ritual of "going to the opera.") Instead of designing his building from the auditorium out, Garnier designed it from the entrance in, as a complicated promenade. As Van Zanten points out, the nub of Garnier's ideas—and by implication, of many other Beaux-Arts architects'—is summed up in the architect's reflection on what the foyer should look like. "But how large should the foyer be? To answer this question we must study how people promenade. . . ." Who, in our present-day landscape of unresponsive grids, does not feel a secret nostalgia at those words?

Robert Hughes, an erstwhile student of architecture, wrote about Louis Kahn in the Autumn, 1974, issue of HORIZON.

The Architect as a Youthful Dreamer

In training to be a public servant, he had his season as a visionary

"Monument to Illustrious Frenchmen," a ziggurat surmounted by a goddess, was conceived in 1833 by a student named Joseph Nicolle.

Ever since Daedelus designed the maze for King Minos, architects have served the mighty of the world—kings, popes, and corporate lords who hope to be remembered for the buildings they commission. Public architecture is their greatest legacy, and the successful practitioner of that art, in the nineteenth century as well as today, could expect to achieve both social and professional prominence. In France, by far the best preparation for architectural distinction was offered by the Ecole des Beaux-Arts. Unfettered by such grim realities as contracts, costs, and questions of where to put the plumbing, budding architects learned to render their visions of glory in minutely detailed ink-and-wash drawings. On this and the following pages are eleven such drawings from a collection of some two hundred recently unearthed at the Ecole des Beaux-Arts and now on display at the Museum of Modern Art in New York. No stone of these projects was ever laid, yet the drawings do more than merely reflect the taste of a bygone era. They embody the rigorous logic at the core of the Beaux-Arts tradition, a logic that underlay even the airiest architectural frivolity. In an age when we so often lament the poverty of imagination in the design of public buildings, there is a special delight in an architectural vision that was thoroughly rational and, at the same time, as grandiose and impractical as castles in a dream.   —M.S.P.

Restoration of the Parthenon by Edouard Loviot, 1881

Railway station by Jean-Camille Formigé, 1876; detail opposite

THE PARTHENON: *Grand-Prix winner Loviot, studying in Rome, re-created the temple—including the murals, the gold and ivory statue of Pallas Athena, and the ornate cornice above—brilliantly colored as the Parthenon was originally.*

RAILWAY STATION: *Passengers were to enter at the right and depart from the left. The classical bull below adorns the façade of the glass and iron shed.*

Pilgrimage church by J. E. A. Duquesne; Grand Prix de Rome, 1897

Casino by Louis-Hippolyte Boileau, 1897

Bridge across a railroad by Emile Vaudremar, 1852

PILGRIMAGE CHURCH: *Surely no pilgrim would ever fail to be inspired by this architectural concoction that combines Florentine, Sienese, and French Gothic elements in a luminous landscape. Its designer was later to become a Harvard professor and city planner in the United States.*

CASINO BY THE SEA: *Boileau was only nineteen when he designed this pleasure palace with its twin beacon towers. The arriving gambler, presumably disembarking from his yacht, would mount a stairway leading through the base of the building and then ascend to the gaming rooms above.*

BRIDGE ACROSS A RAILROAD: *This footbridge, reminiscent of the Rialto in Venice, was intended for some very rich man who had allowed a railroad to cross his private park: the hypothetical tycoon could stand on the bridge and watch the locomotives steam by on the double tracks below.*

OASIS FOUNTAIN: *This tower of stone, vaguely Islamic in mode, would provide water, shelter, and shade for the weary traveler and his camel. In the plan below left, the iron roof appears as a square, which, in the section below right, is seen to be suspended by wires. Canvas curtains form a protective screen against the hot desert winds.*

Fountain for an oasis in the Algerian colonies by Gabriel Ancelet, 1848

ABOVE: *Emmanuel Brune won the Grand Prix de Rome in 1863 with this design for "The Principal Staircase of the Palace of a Sovereign," an unusually specific assignment. The section, slicing through the domed chambers, highlights the colonnaded landing with its equestrian statue at left.*

BELOW: *This prize-winning design for a vast public granary set beside the sea in an exquisite town-scape measures nearly ten feet across. Done in 1797 by Louis-Ambroise Dubut, it was to bear on its façade the proclamation: "Under these vast arcades can Providence maintain equal abundance forever."*

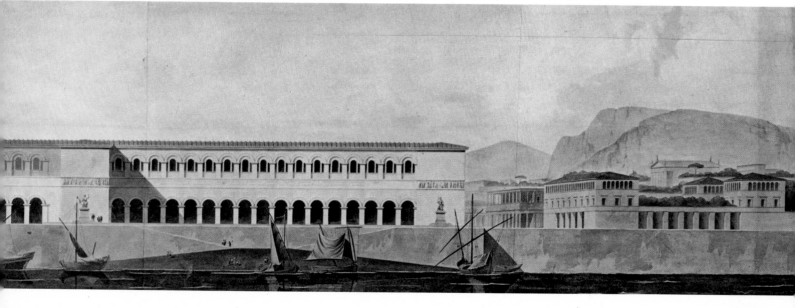

The man at prayer in this miniature is probably Jacques Coeur. His motto, A vaillans cueurs riens inpossible, *is below, with* cueurs *painted out, perhaps by a later owner who wanted no association with the discredited financier.*

How Jacques Coeur Made His Fortune

He made it none too scrupulously,
and lost it at the whim of a much wilier scoundrel than himself

In this carving from Coeur's mansion, a merchant ship sets sail.

One should visit Bourges to see the curious house that Jacques Coeur built, wrote Jules Michelet a century or so ago in his gigantic history of France. It was, he added, "a house full of mysteries, as was Coeur's life." Then, in one of the picturesque asides that make his history such a treasury of unexpected discoveries, he went on to describe that house and the man who built it—the self-made man who played banker to King Charles VII of France, and who bailed out that monarch when his kingdom was at stake; the intrepid man of the world who traded privileges with Moslem sultans, Christian popes, and European princes; the implausibly rich parvenu who, within less than twenty years, parlayed a few counterfeit coins into the largest private fortune in France.

By 1443, when construction of his house started, Coeur was quite possibly the wealthiest man in the world. His new dwelling was to be a monument to his worldly success, and according to one contemporary it was "so richly ornamented, so spacious, and yet, withal, so magnificent, that neither princes of the blood, nor the king himself, had any residence comparable to it." That last point was not lost on Charles VII, as, in the end, Coeur had bitter cause to know.

The house still stands in the cathedral town of Bourges, a short drive south of Paris. It is a unique survival, a memorial as much to a time in history as to the man who built it, for Coeur's life spanned a critical period in the destiny of France. In the last decade of his life the agonizing internecine strife and the bloody slaughter that accompanied the Hundred Years' War were, with his substantial aid, finally brought to an end. The English were thrown back across the Channel, and the land was united as it had not been in living memory.

In the course of those protracted disorders the scrambled authority of feudalism gave way to the more orderly rule of national monarchy, the spirit of chivalry faded before the practical aims of an aspiring bourgeoisie, and the stultifying controls of medieval economy were turning into the growing pains of modern capitalism. To most contemporary eyes such vital changes appeared as a blurred image, like a dissolve in a movie. But Coeur's role in those transitions was so decisive, and he was so perfectly cast for the part he played, that he might well have written the script himself.

It could be said that in Coeur's time double-entry bookkeeping was proving mightier than the sword, for without that instrument of precision and convenience (apparently a fourteenth-century invention), he could hardly have managed his complex affairs. To him, and other businessmen, time—and timekeeping—took on new importance. For time was money made or lost. The easy rhythm of the canonical hours was being replaced by the stern measure of mechanical clocks that counted out the cost of fleeting opportunities, pointed the way to quicker profits, and ticked off interest on loans. And Coeur pressed every advantage. He even used carrier pigeons to bring him advance notice of approaching cargoes so that he could improve his position in the local markets.

From the very beginning Coeur's enterprise was, for better and for worse, closely associated with the interests of his sovereign. Ironically, he first came to public notice in 1429, when, as an associate of the master of the Bourges mint, he was accused of striking coins of inferior alloy. Like so many other functions now considered the exclusive prerogative of government, minting money was then a private concession, albeit by privilege from the king, who took a substantial share of the milling toll as seigniorage, at rates fixed by law. Since no practical system of taxation was yet in force, this was one of the few ways the king could raise money. To meet the demands of the moment, debasing the coinage was approved practice, and the royal "take" could be enhanced by secretly altering the rate of seigniorage —that is, by still further debasing the coinage without advising the public. If the counterfeit was detected, the royal accomplice could disavow the scheme and leave his concessionaires to face the music. And this is what happened to Coeur and his associates in 1429.

Desperate necessities drove Charles VII to practice such duplicity. When he inherited the throne in 1422, the Hundred Years' War was in its eighth grim decade and the fortunes of France were at their lowest ebb. This ill-omened, youthful heir, the tenth child of a madman who disinherited him and of a mother of loose morals who disowned him (it was widely reported that he was a bastard, no matter of shame at the time, but a shadow on his claim to the throne), was holed up in Bourges. An English king reigned in Paris, and English forces occupied all the land from the Channel to the Loire. Philip the Good, the powerful and autonomous duke of Burgundy, tolerated the foreign invader and was allied with him. And Brittany, ever mindful of its own independent traditions, wavered between allegiances.

The years that followed Charles's suc-

The suspicious Charles VII made Coeur his minister of finance, borrowed money from him, and, in the end, ordered his arrest.

cession revolved in a murderous cycle of war and brigandage, pestilence and famine. The king could not afford a standing army, and his military leaders were independent contractors who, between battles with the enemy, roamed the land with their mercenaries, raping, stealing, burning, and killing. Under the circumstances, trade and commerce came to a standstill. Merchants took to the road only if they were armed to the teeth. The great international fairs of Champagne, once vital points of exchange for Europe's traffic, were abandoned as the north-south trade shifted to the sea routes between Flanders and the Mediterranean. France came close to ruin.

The winter of 1428–1429 brought a turning point, or at least a promise of deliverance. The English had laid seige

Macée de Léodépart (whose high hennin indicates family wealth) married Coeur in 1422.

to Orléans, the principal city remaining in Charles's rump of a kingdom. Had Orléans fallen there would have been pitifully little left of that kingdom. The city became a symbol of resistance, while the timid young monarch vacillated in his provincial retreat barely sixty miles away. His mocking enemies dubbed him the "king of Bourges" and anticipated the fall of his petty realm. His treasury was empty; it is said he even borrowed money from his laundress. Only by a miracle could he keep his tottering crown.

The miracle materialized when, as if in direct response to the widely whispered prophecy that an armed virgin would appear and drive the English from the land, Joan of Arc was brought before the king at the château of Chinon where he was then holding court. After grilling the maid for three weeks, the king's counselors decided that she was, as she claimed, divinely appointed by "voices" she had heard to save her king and her country. Somehow, Charles found money to provide her with troops, and the siege of Orléans was lifted. Joan then persuaded her wavering monarch to be crowned at Reims, where Clovis had been baptized. By that ritual the stain of bastardy was automatically removed, and Charles was indisputably the true king of France. It took him eight more years to win Paris from the English, but when he did ride triumphantly into that city, after its sixteen years of foreign occupation, he came as the rightful Christian king.

It was hardly a coincidence that Coeur and his associates were charged with counterfeiting almost immediately after the "miracle" at Orléans, or that Coeur was pardoned of the crime. Charles had most likely met the payroll for Joan's troops with funds provided by the mint's illegal operations, and as party to the crime he saw that Coeur got off easily. At least there is no better explanation.

In any case, soon after his pardon Coeur set out to make his fortune. He formed a new partnership with his old associates at the mint, this time to deal in "every class of merchandise, including that required by the King, Monseigneur the Dauphin, and other nobles, as well as other lines in which they [the partners] can make their profit."

For precedents in this new venture he looked abroad. The basis of Renaissance prosperity, already so conspicuous in Italy, was the carrying trade between East and West. For centuries Venice had fattened on this commerce, to the point where its successful and friendly business relations with Mongols and Moslems alike had encouraged those infidels to close in on the Christian world. Then, as European knighthood took the Cross to the Holy Land, Venetians supplied and equipped their fellow Christians and ferried them to the battle sites at exorbitant rates.

Venice also continued its flourishing trade in arms, armor, and diverse other goods with the Saracens of Egypt and Palestine. When Pope Benedict XII forbade unauthorized trade with the infidel, the merchants of Venice bought up papal authorizations wherever they could and used them as ordinary bills of exchange. With the Fourth Crusade, the "businessman's crusade," the merchants of Venice made a double killing. They dissuaded the debt-burdened knights from their proclaimed purpose of attacking Alexandria, one of Venice's richest markets, and persuaded them to sack the flourishing Christian capital of Constantinople.

Meanwhile, across the Apennines in Tuscany, enterprising merchants were swarming out of Florence into western Europe, collecting contributions to the Crusades as bankers to the Holy See, advancing money to land-poor feudal lords at fantastic interest rates, and with their ready cash buying up the privileges of the towns. During the Hundred Years' War the powerful Bardi and Peruzzi families equipped both French and English armies for the battlefields, prolonging the conflict and taking over the functions of state when it was necessary to secure their accounts. In return for helping Henry III of England with his running expenses, the Florentines

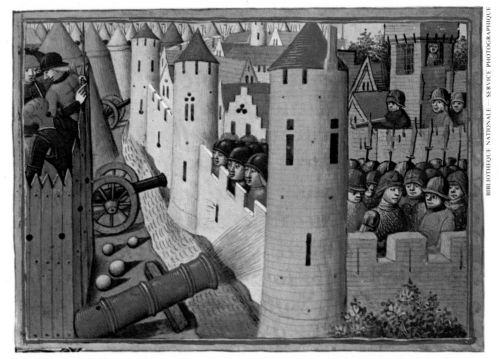

The siege of Orléans (above, a French view of the battle) was lifted in May, 1429, by Joan of Arc. Her troops were paid with coins from the Bourges mint, whose associate master was Jacques Coeur. Shortly after, Coeur was charged with counterfeiting and pardoned by the king.

asked for 120 per cent interest on advances and, when repayment was not prompt, added 60 per cent more. In such a company of greedy Christians, Shylock would have seemed hopelessly ingenuous.

During the most agonizing period of the Hundred Years' War, however, the Florentines had gradually abandoned their commercial colonies in France. Now that his time had come, Coeur moved to fill that vacuum with his own business and, with equal speed, to stake a claim among the markets of the East, so profitably exploited by Venice. His first try at emulating the Venetian merchants was a disaster. In 1432 he journeyed to Damascus, an awkward if not perilous place for Christians to be at the time, buying up spices and other exotic commodities for resale in the home markets of France. When his ship foundered off Corsica he lost literally everything but his shirt. He and his shipmates were stripped clean by the islanders.

He seems to have recovered promptly. He had centered his operations at Montpellier on the Mediterranean coast, the only French port authorized by the pope to deal with the infidel East. He threw himself with bounding determination into the development of the city's facilities, pressing the local authorities to improve its docks, dredge essential canals, construct adequate warehouses, and generally improve the advantages for commerce and navigation—even spending his own money when he had to. As he later wrote the king, he had plans for developing a vast maritime empire under the lily banner of France.

Almost from the moment Charles returned to Paris, Coeur's affairs started to move in a steady counterpoint to the affairs of state. Within a year or two he was installed as *argentier*, receiver of the revenues used to maintain the royal establishment. Since in his capacity as merchant he was also the principal purveyor to that establishment, his position was doubly advantageous—and ambiguous. And since for the most part the court could be accommodated only by long-term credit, both the advantage and the ambiguity were compounded. It must have been quite easy for Coeur to convince himself that what was good for Jacques Coeur was good for France.

A reciprocal rhythm of commissions and benefits, responsibilities and opportunities, honors and profits, increased in tempo for more than a decade. The king may already have been in debt to Coeur even before the royal entry into Paris, and this relationship became more or

In this Book of Hours miniature, the procession to Calvary passes in front of Jacques Coeur's mansion in Bruges. The small figures flanking the doorway are also shown on the opposite page.

less chronic thereafter. The Paris campaign had again exhausted the royal treasury. In an effort to tighten the leaking economy of the state, Charles, possibly advised by his *argentier*, forbade the export of money from his realm except by a special license, which he then granted, apparently exclusively, to Coeur.

In 1440 Charles further recognized Coeur's services by according him patents of nobility. The following year he appointed him *conseilleur du roi*, in effect minister of finance and, as such, adviser in the revision of the nation's tax structure. Charged with assessing and collecting regional taxes, Coeur sometimes received not only his due commissions but gratuities from local representatives who both respected his influence at court and feared his power as a merchant banker. The "states" of Languedoc, for example, of which Montpellier was the principal port, paid him handsomely for his good offices in the interest of their maritime prosperity —canceling his share of their taxes as a matter of course.

The king, meanwhile, with an unprecedented income from the revenues he received, reorganized his military forces into a paid standing army. He was no longer a mere feudal lord but a monarch able to make policy and enforce it, if need be, with cannon—cannon, cast at the foundries of bourgeois manufacturers, that could reduce the proudest knight's castle to rubble. In 1444 Charles arranged a temporary peace with the English, who still held Normandy and Guyenne. It was at the gay spring *pourparlers* on the banks of the Loire by which the peace was negotiated that Charles first spied the indescribably beautiful Agnes Sorel, "the fairest of the fair," whom he shortly afterward made his mistress. As the king's bedmate, Agnes began to use her influence in matters of state, inaugurating a tradition in French history. As it later turned out, this was a fateful development in the life of Jacques Coeur. The immediate consequence of the truce arrangements, however, was that he could now move into the English-held markets in Rouen and Bordeaux as well as across the Channel.

Coeur's influence was already recognized far beyond the shores of France. In 1446 he served as negotiator between the Knights of Rhodes and the sultan of Egypt. Two years later, through the intercession of Coeur's agents, the sultan was persuaded to restore trading privileges to the Venetians, who had for a time been banned from the Arab world. At the same time, Coeur consolidated his own position in the Mediterranean and put a cap on his immense commercial structure. Pope Eugenius IV issued a bull authorizing Coeur to trade for five years in his own right, beyond the privileges enjoyed by the port of Montpellier, with the non-Christian world. With this special authority in his pocket, Coeur shifted the base of his maritime enterprise to Marseilles.

One important matter still needed mending. For all Coeur's good offices and his wide reputation, official relations between France and the Arab world were less cordial than suited his interests. In 1447 he persuaded Charles to agree to a formal pact with Abu-Said-Djacmac-el Daher, sultan of Egypt. The French ambassadors, traveling in Coeur's ships and at his expense, arrived in Egypt "in great state" bearing lavish gifts provided by Coeur in the name of the king. The sultan, in turn, arranged an extravagant reception. Coeur's diplomacy triumphed. Peace between the two lands was agreed upon, and French traders received "most favored nation" privileges in Arab ports.

Aided by the gratitude of the Venetians and the Knights of Rhodes, the friendship of the sultan, the favor of the pope, and the indulgence of his king, Coeur secured unassailable advantages at every important point in the world of his day. "All the Levant he visited with his ships," wrote the duke of Burgundy's chronicler some years later, "and there was not in the waters of the Orient a mast which was not decorated with the *fleur-de-lis*." The maritime empire he created remained for several centuries one of the principal bulwarks of French commerce. To carry on his far-flung, highly diversified operations— they had developed into a virtual monopoly of France's exclusive markets— Coeur employed some three hundred agents and maintained branch offices in Barcelona, Damascus, Beirut, Alexandria, and other strategic centers.

The inventories of his warehouses read like an exaggerated description of Ali Baba's caves. "All the perfumes of Arabia" were carried in stock, and spices and confections from the farthest shores; dyes and colors, cochineal and cinnabar, indigo and saffron—and henna to illuminate the king's manuscripts; materials of fabulous richness and variety, and gems supposedly from the navels of sacred Persian and Indian monkeys, which were mounted in precious metals and considered a universal antidote to human ills. He could provide for the court's most extraordinary or exquisite whim: a coat of mail covered with azure velvet for a Scottish archer of the king's bodyguard; a silver shoulder piece and Turkish buckler for Charles of Orléans; silks and sables for Margaret of Scotland; diamonds to set off the incomparable beauty of Agnes Sorel—they were all to be had, including cold cash for the queen of France herself, who offered up her "great pearl" for security.

In order to put his surplus money to work and to spread his risk, Coeur joined associations that profited from the licensing of fairs (reborn since the temporary truce with England), from speculation in salt, and from the exploitation of copper and silver mines of the Lyonnais and Beaujolais. He had interests in paper and silk factories in Florence. He even invested in three-quarters of two English prisoners of war, each worth a handsome ransom.

The list of his varied enterprises is almost endless. Cash was still in short supply among the nobility, the long war had brought ruin to many lordly tenants, and Charles's fiscal reforms were reducing their income from traditional feudal dues. So Coeur accommodated some of the greatest families of the realm by buying up their manor houses and properties until he held more than thirty es-

Coeur's mansion (above, the main façade) is adorned both inside and out with whimsical vignettes of daily life. The trompe l'oeil *couple below may represent servants watching for their master's return.*

tates, some including whole villages and parishes within their grounds. All told, the complex structure of his myriad affairs, his control of the production, transport, and distribution of goods, his private banking resources, and his secure grasp on essential markets all suggest something like the first vertical trust in history.

So far, nothing belied the motto Coeur was then having chiseled into the stones of his great town house at Bourges—*A vaillans cueurs riens inpossible*, nothing is impossible to the valiant. Coeur's star rose even higher in 1448 when he was sent to Rome by Charles with a select group of ambassadors to help end the "pestilential and horrible" papal schism that for long years had been a great trial to the Church. The French ambassadors entered Rome in a procession of splendor

—their cortege included three hundred richly caparisoned and harnessed Arabian horses—and Pope Nicholas V wrote Charles that not even the oldest inhabitants could remember anything so magnificent.

Coeur promptly took center stage. Through his efforts, the rival pope, Amadeo VIII, duke of Savoy, was finally persuaded to renounce his claim to the papal throne and accept a position in the church hierarchy second only to that of Pope Nicholas V. As a reward, Coeur's privilege of dealing with the non-Christian world was extended indefinitely. He was also given a franchise to carry Christian pilgrims to the Holy Land.

There were some who complained of the outrageous cost of that papal mission from which Coeur gained such honor and profit. Coeur had no doubt paid the bills, but whether from his own purse or from the king's treasury would have been difficult to determine. Coeur's wealth was by now beyond imagining. It was reported that his horses were shod with silver. His table service was of gold and silver. Each year, it was said, his income was greater than that of all the other merchants of France combined. "The king does what he can; Jacques Coeur does what he pleases" was a repeated observation. He might even be in league with the devil, they began to say.

Jacques Coeur had indeed reached a singular, and perilous, eminence.

How rich Coeur really was and what resources he could command came out in the years immediately following. The time had come, Charles decided, to break the truce with the English and to push them out of France altogether. To launch and maintain the campaign, however, Charles needed more money than he could find in the royal coffers, and he turned to Coeur for help. Coeur responded by dredging every sou he could manage from the resources available to him and by stretching his almost inexhaustible credit to the limit. By one means or another, he turned over to the king, at the very minimum, two hundred thousand ecus, a sum equal to more than one-fifth of the kingdom's annual tax revenues.

He also took to the field at the king's side. In the victorious procession that entered Rouen on November 10, 1449, Coeur rode in the company of Charles; mounted on a white charger, he was clothed in velvet and ermine and wore a sword embellished with gold and precious stones.

Coeur was now about fifty-five years old. For some twenty years he had enjoyed increasing wealth and prestige. Then, suddenly, the wheel of fortune changed direction. Three months after the ceremonies at Rouen, Agnes Sorel died in childbirth, after having been delivered of the king's fourth child. Rumors spread that she had been poisoned. Almost automatically, a cabal of debtors formed to point a finger at the king's *argentier*, the "money man" of almost magical faculties, who was known to be one of the executors of Agnes's will. To convict Coeur of murder would serve to disembarrass the king and every important member of the court from the claims of their common creditor.

Charles was quick to play his part. One week in July, 1451, he expressed his gratitude to Coeur for his many services; the next week he issued an order for his arrest. Supported by his most recent favorites, the king confronted Coeur with a long list of indictments, starting with the poisoning charge and going back over the years to the counterfeiting charge of 1429, set aside so long ago by the pleasure and the convenience of Charles VII.

No sooner were the dungeon doors closed behind Coeur than "the vultures of the court" started picking away at the estate he could no longer protect. The nobility of France swarmed about the tottering house of Jacques Coeur to redeem their own fortunes from his

Agents of the king arrest Coeur on July 31, 1451, and charge him with a list of crimes that include the poisoning of Agnes Sorel.

disgrace. The trial that followed was a mockery. With his enemies as both prosecutors and judges he never had a chance. Even though his accusers confessed that the charge of poisoning Agnes Sorel was false, and the pope pleaded for clemency and justice in the case, Coeur was shunted for several years from prison to prison.

Finally, in May, 1453, at Poitiers, when he was threatened with torture, he issued a statement that led his judges to condemn him, banish him, and confiscate his properties. By a remarkable coincidence, on the day of Coeur's sentence the sorely tried city of Constantinople fell, this time once and for all, to the Turks. It was the end of an era. Less than a week later, the con-

Coeur makes his amende honorable, *begging God, King Charles, and the courts for mercy.*

victed man made an *amende honorable*: kneeling, bareheaded, before a large crowd and holding a ten-pound wax torch in his hands, he begged mercy of God, king, and the courts.

One more adventure remained. For almost a year and a half after his trial, Coeur was kept imprisoned in France, in spite of his banishment, while most of his holdings were seized and sold off. Then, in the autumn of 1454, he managed to escape. Aided by several of his faithful agents, he crossed the Rhone out of France and fled to Rome, where the pope received him with honor. He never returned to France, nor to the house that was his pride.

But he did take to the sea one last time. He arrived in Rome at a crucial moment in the history of the Church and of Western civilization. All Christendom had been shaken by the fall of Constantinople less than two years earlier and felt threatened by further advances of the Ottoman hordes. In the summer of 1456, Coeur, sixty years old and "toiled with works of war," set forth in command of a fleet dispatched by Pope Calixtus III to help retake Constantinople. On the twenty-fifth of November, on the island of Chios, his *vaillant coeur* was stopped, possibly by wounds he suffered in battle.

As he lay dying, Coeur sent one last appeal to Charles, begging the king to show consideration for his children. At this point Charles could afford to be indulgent. In an act of royal compassion he conceded that since "the said Coeur was in great authority with us and rich and abounding in this world's goods and ennobled in his posterity and line ... it pleases us to have pity on [his children]," and ordained that what might be salvaged from their father's estate, including the house at Bourges, be returned to them.

It was, after all, little enough for him to do, and in the end Coeur had an ironic revenge. The thought of poisoning continued to haunt the king. Four years later, fearing he might be poisoned by his own son, he refused to eat, and died of starvation.

Agnes Sorel, mistress to Charles VII, appears as the Virgin in a diptych panel painted by Jean Fouquet in about 1450 — the year of her death — and commissioned by Etienne Chevalier, one of the executors of her will.

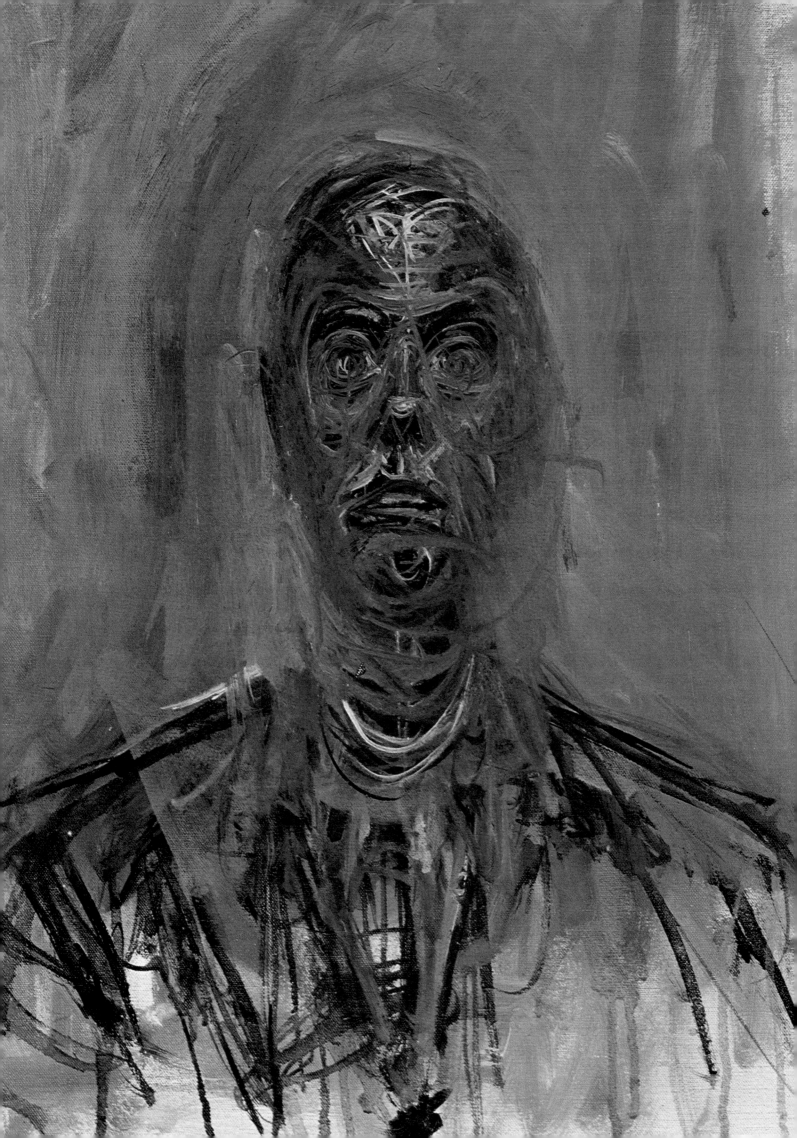

"To Render What the Eye Sees Is Impossible"

Concluding that complexities of vision made his artistic goals unattainable, Giacometti thought himself a failure. A decade after his death, most people think otherwise

Alberto Giacometti's place in art history is secure; indeed, in the decade since his death he has become a modern classic, a standard museum attraction. But defining his importance is not easy. He did not launch any revolutionary "ism." He has had very little influence, except perhaps as a model of probity. Today he is frequently referred to as an expressionist—fair enough if one thinks only of certain aspects of the work of his last phase. Forty years ago, however, when he was making what he called "objects without pedestals and without value, to be thrown away," he was regarded as the official court sculptor of the Paris surrealists and their dictator, André Breton. At one point he was a first-rate cubist. In some ways he was scarcely modern at all: he complained regularly, for instance, about the difficulty of doing a human nose "after nature," and he was unabashedly interested in returning to the ancient Mediterranean notion that man was the proper subject of art.

During the last phase of his career Giacometti was typecast as an apostle of existentialism, a victim of anxiety, an incarnation of the Outsider—in short, one of our representative modern *misérables*. Today, ten years after his death, he is sometimes still cast in that role, and not without reason. He was often in the company of the existentialist pope Jean Paul Sartre and the counterculture rebel Jean Genêt, and he was something of a real-life version of Roquentin, the character in Sartre's *La nausée* who is transfixed by the sheer "otherness" of things. Moreover, the best-known Giacometti sculptures—the ravaged, desolate figures produced after World War II—imply estrangement in many ways. They stare. They are as thin as matchsticks. They are earnestly futile. The men stride masterfully off toward nowhere; the naked, hysterical women, thighs tightly locked, stand and wait like unemployed caryatids.

Evidence of alienation, or at least of a strange sentiment of loneliness when confronted by the physical world, can also be found in some of the stories Giacometti told about his perceptual adventures. For instance, late one night on his way home to No. 46 rue Hippolyte-Maindron, on the southern edge of Montparnasse, he was wrenched by an extraordinary anguish. "I felt," he said later, "that I was changed into a dog, a dog of my quarter sniffing the ground with his muzzle, a ground I saw in front of me with ghastly clarity."

HENRI CARTIER-BRESSON—MAGNUM

Arranging an exhibit in 1961, Giacometti paces among his creations. At left is his tall bronze Walking Man I, *executed the previous year. Nearby stands a ghostly, enlongated nude, and on the floor are three busts of his brother Diego, who also served as the model for the oil portrait opposite.*

By ROY McMULLEN

HEAD OF A MAN II (Diego), 1964: detail

SELF-PORTRAIT, 1921

Born into a family of artists in southern Switzerland, Giacometti began drawing, painting, and sculpturing at an early age. The self-portrait above, done when he was twenty, is in the style of Cézanne, whom he greatly admired. A few years later he sketched his family, below, at their summer house. His father, an accomplished painter, is at an easel, his mother sews, and the artist chisels a stone.

Oil sketch of the Giacometti family, 1925

There was another time, according to his own testimony, when everyone in the Paris subway looked stone dead. And one evening in the Brasserie Lipp, he glanced up from his table and noticed that the waiter's head had popped out of the stream of time, like a frozen shot in a film: he was "leaning over me, mouth open, with no connection at all with the preceding moment, nor with the following moment, mouth open, eyes fixed."

Sometimes the transformations involved objects. One day a portfolio left on a chair in his bedroom abruptly acquired a new mode of existence, a mixture of uncanny solitude, vividness, and negative gravity. "I had the impression," he reported to Genêt, "that I could take away the chair without causing the portfolio to change its place. It had a place of its own, a weight of its own, even a silence of its own."

The oddness of such experiences went with an oddness in the man himself. By middle age he seemed about to be metamorphosed into a dusty plaster cast; his bushy hair was gray, his haggard, mobile face —the face of a sad Italian mime—was gray, even his lips and teeth were gray. In 1938 he had been run down by a drunken motorist, and as a result he walked with a slight hobble, like the god Vulcan. His habits were thoroughly Bohemian. He occupied his small, dark studio in Montparnasse from 1927, when he was twenty-six, until his death in 1966; and each year the clutter grew deeper. He was indifferent to fame and money; he enjoyed the company of social outcasts, particularly the prostitutes and beggar women of his quarter.

Odd, too, for a successful artist was his talk about the utter hopelessness of his efforts to sculpture, paint, and draw; toward the end of his life he dismissed his career as "thirty-five years of dishonesty." Another day or two of trying, he would say, and then he would be ready to give up forever. Anyway, he would argue, statues and pictures were not nearly as important as a lot of other things in the world; if he ever got caught in a burning house with a Rembrandt and a cat, he would save the cat. People who noticed that he was a reasonably prolific artist thought this despair over his work was a joke. Yet his models—his mother, his wife Annette, trapped friends, and above all his brother Diego—testified to his cycles of depression and his habit of undoing, like Penelope, what he had just done.

Clearly, then, if we define "existentialist" in the loose, mournful terms that caught the popular imagination of the 1950's, Giacometti had what it took to play the role in which he was cast. But he was not just a professional pessimist, and certainly not just a Left Bank period phenomenon. He was a fiercely conscientious man who struggled with problems that have been ignored—or regarded as themes for reactionaries—by most of the major artists of the twentieth century. His achievement is probably best summarized as a long, fitful, painful evolution toward a compassionate yet unsentimental humanism and a unique style of realism.

At Stampa, the village in Italian-speaking Switzerland where he was born and raised, he was surrounded by reproductions and original works of art. His father, Giovanni Giacometti, was a respected impressionist painter; his father's cousin, Augusto, was a pioneer abstractionist, and his godfather, Cuno Amiet, a postimpressionist follower of Gauguin. By the time he was ten Alberto was already accomplished enough to produce his own sketched version of a Dürer engraving, *Knight, Death, and the Devil*; at twelve he painted his first oil, a still life with apples; and at thirteen he did his first sculpture, a bust of Diego. In 1920, at the age of nineteen, he went to Italy for an artistic grand tour. "In Venice first," he wrote, "where I spent my days looking mostly at the Tintorettos. . . . To my great regret, on the day I left Venice, Tintoretto was a little dethroned by the Giottos in Padua, and he in turn some months later by Cimabue at Assisi." He lived in Rome for nine months, painting and sculpturing a little, reading Sophocles and Aeschylus, and mostly visiting museums and churches: "I wanted to see everything. . . ." In 1922 he settled in Paris and for three years was a pupil of the sculptor Antoine Bourdelle, a poetic ex-disciple of Rodin who urged students to become "mathematicians in form and musicians in proportion."

During this formative period Giacometti acquired the habit of making pencil copies of the drawings, paintings, and sculpture of past masters. It was a habit he never abandoned. There were times, in fact, when the habit almost dominated him, when he felt that he was about to penetrate some mighty secret by forcing his hand to follow the movements of long-dead hands. In 1965, a few months before he died, he described his vivid memories of those early years:

Suddenly I see myself in Rome at the Borghese Gallery copying a Rubens, one of the great discoveries of the day, but at this same moment I see myself in all my past: at Stampa near the window around 1914 concentrating on a copy of a Japanese print, every detail of which I can describe . . . and then a Pintoricchio surges up, and all the frescoes of the Quattrocento painters in the Sistine Chapel; I see myself four years later coming back in the evening to my Paris studio and going through books and copying this or that piece of Egyptian sculpture or a Carolingian miniature.

As well as intimately acquainting himself with the great art of the past, Giacometti absorbed the work of contemporary artists; in Paris he learned much about intellectual clarity, geometric discipline, and the rhythmic possibilities of light and shade from the cubist sculptors Henri Laurens and Jacques Lipchitz. He studied the slender forms of Constantin Brancusi and the rough textures of Rodin, who was almost a contemporary, having died in 1917.

The combination of family influence, study of great works, and proximity to the modernists in France could easily have led to a fairly safe career as either a conventional traditionalist or a conventional modernist. That Giacometti finally became neither was the result of his obsessive preoccupation with visual perception, a preoccupation that, at first, threatened to undo him psychologically.

In Rome in 1921 he began work on two busts. Then suddenly, he later recalled, he found that he could not focus properly: "I was lost, everything escaped me, the head of the model before me became like a cloud, vague and undefined." He demolished the busts. In Paris the next year the trouble began again. In the drawing classes he attended at the Montparnasse Académie de la Grande-Chaumière, he felt that he was too close to the model. When he concentrated on details of the human anatomy, they quickly became monstrous; the tip of a nose, for example, dissolved into "little more than granules moving over a deep black void," and the space across the nostrils loomed at him "like the Sahara, without end."

By 1925 he was convinced he was heading toward a psychological catastrophe, and in the hope of saving himself he decided to abandon

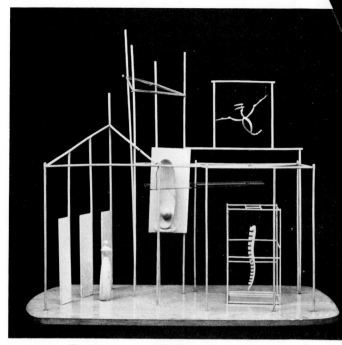

THE PALACE AT 4 A.M., 1932–33

After Giacometti went to live in Paris in the twenties, he began to experiment with abstract sculpture, often using forms derived from primitive art. A carved wooden dish from Oceania, for instance, inspired the smoothly concave Spoon Woman. In the thirties Giacometti often exhibited with the Paris surrealists, showing works with ambiguous and sometimes menacing themes, like Woman with Her Throat Cut. The Palace at 4 A.M. is like a surrealist dream: the woman's figure, Giacometti once said, represents his mother "as she appears in my earliest memories."

WOMAN WITH HER THROAT CUT, 1932

SPOON WOMAN, 1926

CITY SQUARE, 1948

Matchstick men stride across a bare plaza, above, their paths leading inexorably past an unnoticed woman who stands alone in the center. These city dwellers are aloof and inaccessible, like the bronze figure opposite. Although Giacometti insisted he was only trying to reproduce what he saw, his figures—and such grotesqueries as the heads and dog below—appear to reflect his own sense of alienation.

NOSE, 1947

DOG, 1951

HEAD OF A MAN ON A ROD, 1947

live models and work only from memory or imagination. During the next ten years, neglecting his painting and drawing, he produced a miscellaneous collection of avant-garde sculptures. There were semiabstract idols, some reminiscent of primitive African sculpture; there were vaguely symbolic surrealist objects, like *Woman with Her Throat Cut,* and cagelike constructions, notably *The Palace at 4 A.M.* (both page 89), the result of Giacometti's desire to represent what he termed "a sense of the whole, a structure, also a sharpness I saw, a kind of skeleton in space." Finally there were macabre creations like a *Cubist Head* of 1934–35, which, despite its forceful geometry, recalls an Aztec death's-head.

But he could not remain indifferent to the reality of the human figure, and in 1935 he began to work again from a live model. His idea was to do "one or two studies from nature, just enough to understand the construction of a head," but the outcome was five years of daily struggle and defeat: "Nothing was as I had imagined. A head (I quickly abandoned figures . . .) became for me an object completely unknown and without dimensions. Twice a year I began two heads, always the same ones, never completing them."

In 1940 he tried again to do without a model, relying this time on his ability to recall his visual perceptions. The result was another disaster: "The sculptures became smaller and smaller, yet their dimensions revolted me, and tirelessly I began again, only to end several months later at the same point."

He spent the last three years of World War II in Switzerland, still struggling unsuccessfully to overcome the small scale of his work. When he returned to Paris in 1945 his entire production for those three years was said to fit into six matchboxes; this may be an exaggeration, but the sculptures were alarmingly tiny. Then, apparently through the discipline of drawing, he got his sense of scale under control. In the late forties he began the creation of the tall, slim, rough bronzes, the pencil or pen sketches, and the paintings, usually portraits, that were to occupy him for the remaining twenty years of his life. And at about the same time, through the sale of his work, he emerged from the financial difficulties that had for a while forced him and his brother Diego, an able artisan in bronze, to earn their living by making lamps, vases, chairs, and other furnishings for a Paris interior decorator.

Despite continual new beginnings and frequent failures, Giacometti produced enough work to have successful one-man shows in Paris and New York. A German critic, Willy Rotzler, wrote of a visit to the artist's studio in the spring of 1950:

He was in the middle of extremely intensive and fruitful work on his skinny, fantastically elongated standing figures. His ground-floor room was filled with them in all sizes, states, and materials. Giacometti, cigarette never absent from his left hand, walked restlessly up and down, searching like an animal in a cage. Then he carefully unwrapped the damp, clayey cloths from the figure on which he was currently working. Hesitantly at first, then as if an idea had unexpectedly occurred to him, kneading hurriedly, gouging valleys, building up ridges and knolls, his fingers crawled up and down the figure on its wire core.

Among the major pieces of sculpture of this postwar period are *Man Pointing,* a proud but haggard figure made in 1947; *City Square,*

CHARIOT, 1950

THE ARTIST'S MOTHER, 1950

a bronze slab across which five lonely figures stride (page 90); the *Chariot* (page 91); a series of female figures; a series of men walking; a number of portraits, executed between 1954 and 1964, of his wife Annette; and a number of portraits of his brother Diego. To be in a room with some of these objects is to be in a place that is unmistakably inhabited, as if by living people. It is also to be in an atmosphere heavy with anxiety. Yet Giacometti frequently denied, especially during his last years, that his aim was to suggest any particular psychological reality, such as loneliness. He claimed that he was concerned exclusively with visible reality—optical data. But can we accept this assertion?

Certainly we cannot accept it without some commonsense qualifications. To begin with, what he sometimes called his "vision of reality" was plainly affected by his knowledge of the art of the past. His gaunt bronzes, although in no sense replicas, recall Egyptian, Archaic Greek, Cycladic, and Etruscan sculpture. The usually strict frontality and the hypnotic stare of his painted figures remind one of Sumerian worshipers, Byzantine mosaics, and the large-eyed Egyptian mummy portraits of the Roman era.

We can also assume that his vision was conditioned by his technique. Whereas an Easter Islander or a Michelangelo carves away waste material from a block until he has the image he wants, Giacometti built up his most characteristic images by adding blobs of clay to an armature. Instead of tools he used his hands, in particular his gouging thumbs. (He took much the same kind of approach in his drawings and paintings, where the images are built up by repetitive strokes, elaborating the basic "armature.")

Certainly his private fantasies and emotional experiences entered into his sculpture. The Giacometti who was changed into a sniffing Montparnasse mongrel, for instance, exists in bronze. Made into sculptures, too, although in a less precise way, were his visions of the zombies of the Paris subway and the waiter at the Brasserie Lipp. The bronze *Chariot*, a slender nude standing on a two-wheeled platform, is partly the metamorphosis of a pharmacy wagon that was wheeled around his room when he was in the hospital after his accident in 1938.

There is much about Giacometti's work, however, that cannot be explained by art-historical or personal factors. He actually was concerned with *seeing* in the ordinary sense of the word, and he did, in fact, have difficulty with perception. Specifically, he seems to have had trouble with the visual constancies, the perceptual processes that lead us to disregard, or to compensate for, the information on our retinas and thus finally to see what we think makes sense.

Size constancy, for instance, as we all have learned and probably forgotten, enables our brains to adjust for the fact that the retinal image of an object halves with each doubling of the distance of the object from the eye. Without such psychological tampering with optical reality, we would see mountains as molehills, molehills as mountains, and a friend across the room as an elf. Precisely this sort of aberration appears to have afflicted Giacometti all his life. The evidence is not only in his Sahara-size noses and Lilliputian nymphs, but also in his paintings of relatively conventional subjects. One of his portraits of his mother in her parlor shows her pathetically dwindled;

Gray Meant Trouble

Painting from life was an all-absorbing if often frustrating activity for Giacometti. For his models (such as his mother, who appears in the portrait opposite), posing was an exercise in patience and fortitude. His good friend James Lord, an American writer living in Paris, has left a revealing record of his eighteen days as Giacometti's model in 1964. Although Giacometti planned to finish in no more than a day or two, it soon became clear that the portrait was going to take much longer than that. By the twelfth sitting, Lord began to despair: "I sat there, immobile, silent, perspiring, staring him in the eye.... What alone existed with a life of its own was his indefatigable, interminable struggle via the act of painting to express in visual terms a perception of reality that had happened to coincide momentarily with my head." They finally agreed on a deadline: only four more sittings would be allowed. Early in their sessions Lord had noticed that every time Giacometti dipped his brush in grayish pigment it meant that he was "yet again starting to undo what he had done." At the last sitting, when Giacometti once again made for the gray, Lord cannily asked if he could rest. Giacometti painted only a few more strokes. Then, as Lord tells it, "I stood up, went behind him, and looked at the painting. It was superb.... Never before had the picture looked just as it did then, and it had never looked better." The artist's opinion was more guarded: "It's only the beginning of what it could be. But that's something, anyway."

PORTRAIT OF JAMES LORD, 1964

Sculpturing a bust of Annette, 1962

In his Paris studio, above, Giacometti puts what seem to be the finishing touches on a portrait bust of his wife, Annette. The bust is similar to the bronze head opposite, which he completed about the same time. Diego in profile, below, is one of the thousands of portraits Giacometti made of his brother over the years. He once said, in fact, that he had sculptured their heads so often that when he did a head from memory it usually turned out looking like Diego or Annette.

HEAD OF DIEGO, 1954

in another she seems about to disappear altogether. In a desperate attempt to control such effects, he painted red marks on his studio floor to indicate the exact positions of himself and his model.

Our brains also adjust for the angles of view that produce "distortions" of shape in the retinal images. If it were not for this, we would see square tables as diamond-shaped and round glasses as oval, and we would be baffled by the thinness of people seen from an angle. Giacometti insisted that he actually saw people who looked strangely thin, who seemed to have part of their mass eroded by space. Obviously, the attenuated forms of his bronze men and women cannot be explained completely by the failure of shape constancy; in fact, Giacometti once said he wished to convey the lightness of people in motion by making his figures so thin. But his reliance on uninterpreted retinal data may have contributed to their distortion.

Although we can never know exactly what Giacometti saw, it is clear that through his observations and the discipline of drawing, he developed an unusual capacity that the critic Reinhold Höhl has termed "absolute eye," analogous to absolute pitch in music. As Höhl described it:

Giacometti's optical memory became so exact with time that, when he resumed work on a canvas he may have begun months earlier, he knew, to the centimeter, whether or not the model was sitting the same distance from him as in the earlier session. This ability brought experience with it, and a very personal way of seeing things: he saw nothing and no one life-size.

Giacometti himself once said: "Life-size does not exist. It is a meaningless concept. Life-size is at the most your own size—but you don't see yourself."

His "trouble" with size and shape constancies, then, was not attributable to some peculiar eye malady; it was the result of his commitment to the problem of reconciling art, reality, and visual perception. He seems to have felt that conventional ways of looking, fostered in part by sculptors and painters, had finally, after centuries of acceptance, become barriers between ourselves and what is not ourselves: "The gap between any work of art and the immediate reality of anything has become too great," he once wrote, "and I have reached a point where nothing except reality interests me." He was ready, therefore, to run the risk of trying to start the whole business of seeing and depicting over again, from scratch. He was often quite explicit about what he was trying to do. In 1957 he expressed his dilemma to Jean Genêt: "You have got to paint exactly what is in front of you. And, in addition, you have got to produce a painting."

He knew that the problem he had set himself was finally insoluble. In 1964, without his usual irony, he admitted that "to render what the eye really sees is impossible." Yet he continued to work productively, remaining a remarkably optimistic *misérable*. A few months before his death he sized himself up in his notebook with characteristically cheerful disenchantment: "I don't know, am I a comedian, a swindler, an idiot, or a very scrupulous fellow? I only know I've got to keep trying to draw a nose after nature."

Roy McMullen, a free-lance writer who lives in Paris, has written articles about history, art, and philosophy for HORIZON. *His most recent book, published last fall, is* The Mona Lisa: The Picture and the Myth.

TRAVELS
INTO
SEVERAL REMOTE NATIONS
OF THE WORLD
By LEMUEL
GULLIVER

Jonathan Swift,
master satirist that he was, detested mankind.
He wrote in the stubborn hope
that people could be stung, lashed, and
jabbed into better sense

ILLUSTRATED FOR HORIZON BY GEOFFREY MOSS

Children have always loved *Gulliver's Travels*. Yet adjusting it for the children's book market has always been an awkward problem. What to leave in? What to take out? Some things clearly have to go. A sophisticated child might be more amused than shocked by the spectacle of Gulliver extinguishing the fire in the Lilliputian imperial palace by urinating on it. But there is something considerably more dubious, when the hero travels on to the land of the gigantic Brobdingnagians, about the maid of honor who puts him, stripped naked, "astride upon one of her nipples"; or in Balnibarbi, on the next voyage, about the scientist whose project is "to reduce human excrement to its original food, by separating the several parts, removing the tincture which it receives from the gall, making the odour exhale, and scumming off the saliva"; or finally, in Houyhnhnmland, the country of noble horses, about the activities of the repulsive, apelike animals called Yahoos, whose regular pursuits almost all involve the genitoexcretory region. Some editors have given up and left out "A Voyage to the Houyhnhnms" and "A Voyage to Laputa," thereby cutting the book approximately in half.

The whole question would have profoundly irritated Jonathan Swift. He did not like children much, and he certainly did not write his book for them. "Not to be fond of children, nor let them come near me hardly" was one of a series of resolutions he made in 1699, at the age of thirty-two, to guide him in later life. *A Modest Proposal for Preventing the Children of Poor People from Being a Burden to their Parents or the Country* (1729), probably his best-known work next to *Gulliver*, could hardly have been written by a man who loved kids. Its central suggestion—that a hundred thousand one-year-olds be butchered annually and sold as meat—was, of course, savagely ironical, but there is something chilling about his having thought of it at all.

Swift wanted *Gulliver's Travels* to reach a broad public. For its first two books he hit upon an easy but enchant-

ing device. As every schoolboy knows, his hero wanders first to a country where the entire populace is miniature, on a scale of one inch to a foot, and subsequently to a country where everyone towers over him in the reverse proportion. A good deal of the fascination of the voyages to Lilliput and Brobdingnag depends simply on working out in meticulous detail the consequences of these disparities in size. In Lilliput, Gulliver needs six hundred mattresses to make him a bed. Every day he consumes six whole beeves, forty sheep, and enough bread and wine for a battalion. A troop of horses performs maneuvers on his stretched-out handkerchief; three hundred tailors make

The amiable Swift in a serious mood

him a suit of clothes, taking his measurements with a plumb line.

Conversely, in Brobdingnag, Gulliver has horrifying encounters with enormous rats, birds, dogs, and the queen's dwarf—who is thirty feet tall. He contrives a comb out of stubs of hair from the king's beard and entertains the royal party by playing a tune on a sixty-foot spinet, scampering back and forth along the huge keyboard socking it with mallets. Showing off in front of his "little nurse," Glumdalclitch, he tries to jump a heap of Brobdingnagian cow dung but lands "just in the middle up to my knees."

This is all good fun, but it is not long before bright children and adults become aware that there is more here

than the old diversion of viewing a scene first through one end of a telescope and then through the other. There is an irony of perspective at work. The civilizations of both the Lilliputians and the Brobdingnagians closely resemble that of eighteenth-century Europe, but Gulliver sees things he never noticed at home in England. In Lilliput nearly everything seems petty; in Brobdingnag nearly everything seems gross.

The Lilliputians have a high opinion of themselves. They describe their leader as "most mighty Emperor of Lilliput, delight and terror of the universe, whose dominions extend five thousand *blustrugs* . . . to the extremities of the globe." That turns out to be about twelve miles. The emperor's inclination toward pomp and circumstance goes easily awry: when he has his army parade between Gulliver's legs "with drums beating, colours flying, and pikes advanced," as if beneath a triumphal arch, some of "the younger officers" cannot help taking a quick look at the Man-Mountain's crotch; and "to confess the truth, my breeches were at that time in so ill a condition, that they afforded some opportunities for laughter and admiration." Later, Gulliver reports, a court scandal threatens to erupt over a rumor that the wife of Flimnap, the Lilliputian treasurer, "had taken a violent affection for my person; and . . . that she once came privately to my lodging." Gulliver elaborately denies any intrigue with the five-inch beauty, not in terms of physical impossibility, but in terms of his own moral rectitude.

That the Lilliputians are picayune in spirit as well as in body becomes absurdly clear as the story unfolds. They have their political parties and intrigues, and their disputes with the neighboring kingdom of Blefuscu, which is peopled by the same species of little creatures. The great issue between Lilliput's two political parties is whether high-heeled shoes are better or worse than low; between Lilliput and Blefuscu, whether eggs should be broken at the larger end or the smaller. Party feeling is so intense that the High-Heelers "will neither eat

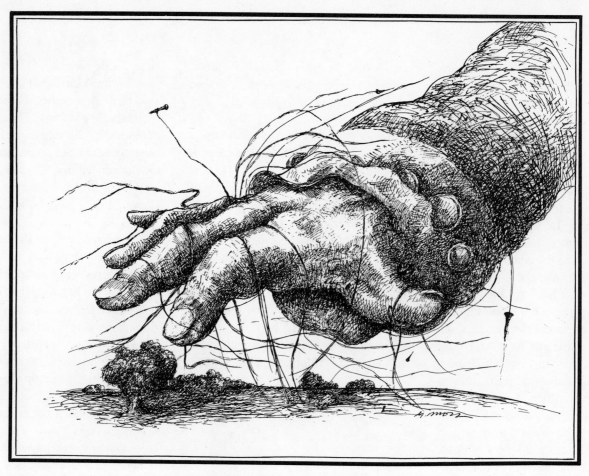

nor drink, nor talk" with the Low-Heelers, who, however, have the good fortune to be in favor at court. Meanwhile, "a bloody war has been carried on between the two empires for six and thirty moons" over the Big-Endian–Little-Endian controversy. The Lilliputians have already lost some thirty thousand of their best sailors and soldiers, but they console themselves with reports that the body count is even higher on the other side. Swift's contemporaries must have chuckled over this sort of thing when they realized that the differences between Whigs and Tories, or between England and France in the recently concluded War of the Spanish Succession (1701–1714), were likewise of debatable importance.

Swift, at any rate, thought so. Although the most stimulating chapter of his life was his service to the Tory government as pamphleteer and publicist from 1708 to 1714, he had earlier been a Whig, and he believed that among men of good sense and good will party distinctions should not be dominant. A confidant, up to a point, of Robert

"I attempted to rise, but was not able to stir: for as I happened to lie on my back, I found my arms and legs were strongly fastened on each side to the ground; and my hair, which was long and thick, tied down in the same manner."

—LILLIPUT

Harley, first earl of Oxford and Queen Anne's chief minister, Swift exercised his pen against John Churchill, first duke of Marlborough, who he thought was prosecuting the war for his own advantage. He also effectively defended the Tory maneuverings that led to the end of "this ruinous war" (as Oxford called it) and the Peace of Utrecht.

Swift had arrived at this high level of political influence almost entirely through his power as a writer. Born in Ireland in 1667, to a recently widowed English woman of little means, he was educated, rather parsimoniously, by an uncle. Reminiscing a generation later about Kilkenny College, his secondary school, he spoke of "confinement ten hours a day to nouns and verbs, the terror of the rod, the bloody noses, and broken shins." He does not seem to have been much happier at Dublin's Trinity

College, where he was an underachiever and barely squeaked by with a bachelor's degree in 1685. Nevertheless, Sir William Temple, the distinguished retired diplomat who took him on as private secretary three years later, found the young man altogether competent and reliable. Swift was temporarily content at the Temple manor, Moor Park, in Surrey. Sir William was a bookish man and a polished writer; the household atmosphere was pleasantly urbane; the service and food were excellent.

There was, moreover, an attractive outlet for the strongly didactic temper that Swift displayed all his life. The family favorite was a pretty, black-haired little girl named Hester Johnson, whose connection with the Temples is not entirely clear but who may have been Sir William's illegitimate daughter. Among his other duties, Swift acted as her tutor. Thus began a relationship that was to last until she died in 1728. Stella, as he called her, became a kind of Galatea to Swift's Pygmalion: he shaped her into a beautiful and accomplished woman, and within the stern limits that he set

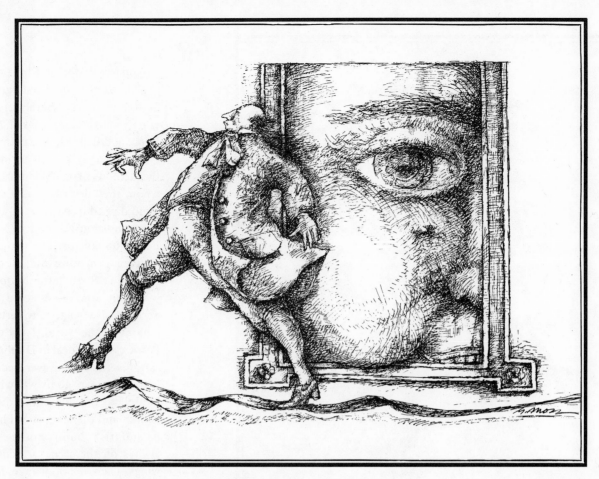

himself, he loved her. But for her, it was never to be quite enough.

Swift's service with Temple was interrupted in 1694 when he joined the Anglican priesthood. For the next two years he performed, without enthusiasm, the duties of a parson in an Irish country parish. The church for him was simply a respectable living. In theology he leaned more toward skepticism than dogma, but he never doubted that an established church was necessary for the ordering of civilized society; it was, in effect, an arm of the government.

Before he returned to Moor Park in 1696, he appears to have fallen in love with a deacon's daughter named Jane Waring; he called her Varina. There exists an extraordinary love letter, a kind of ultimatum, in which he exhorts her to join him in "the joys that accompany a true, honourable, unlimited love." She hesitated too long, and he went morosely back to Surrey. It has been supposed by some biographers that Swift's "rejection" by Varina permanently damaged his capacity for a fully developed sexual relationship with

*"*Several of the country shows . . . exceed all nations I have known, both for dexterity and magnificence. I was diverted with none so much as that of the rope-dancers, performed upon a slender white thread, extended about two foot, and twelve inches from the ground.*"*
—LILLIPUT

any woman. The fact is, however, that when a few years later she let him know she was ready, he slapped her down with a letter so frigidly ferocious that doubts arise about the sincerity of his original proposal. Something was working in this proud young man, probably from the time of his fatherless boyhood, to make normal sexual expression impossible.

In the meantime Swift had begun his writing career. It started with poetry, and although he would continue to write verse all his life, the modern reader is likely to sympathize with John Dryden, a distant cousin, who is reported to have said, after reading an early effort, "Cousin Swift, you will never be a poet." In any event, his true genius declared itself in prose, for it was after coming back to Moor Park that he wrote *A Tale of a Tub* and *The Battle of*

the Books. They are hardly read today by anyone except graduate students, but both are studded with passages of dazzling invention and wit.

In *The Battle of the Books* young Swift took up his literary lance in defense of his patron, Sir William, who had bogged down in a dispute over the relative merits of ancient and modern authors. As part of a Homeric burlesque advancing the superiority of the ancients, Swift wrote the famous fable of the spider (the moderns) and the bee (the ancients). The bee has by far the best of it, as an eminent producer of both honey and wax—sweetness and light. In passing, Swift got off a jab or two at Cousin Dryden, who appears as a warrior for the moderns in a helmet "nine times too large for the head." It was one of the first indications of something many were to learn: Jonathan Swift never forgot an insult.

A Tale of a Tub is a learned but disrespectful, if not scurrilous, allegory on the subject of organized religion. For many years afterward—the book was not published until 1704—Swift was in

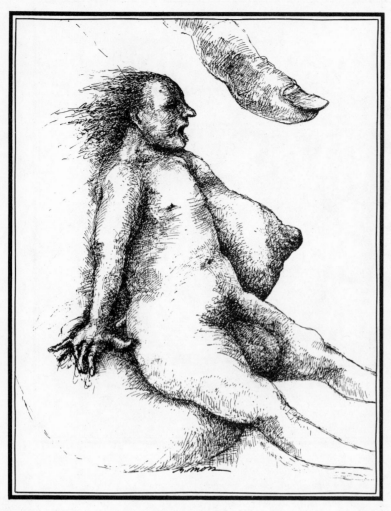

"The handsomest among these Maids of Honour, a pleasant frolicsome girl of sixteen, would sometimes set me astride upon one of her nipples, with many other tricks, wherein the reader will excuse me for not being over particular."
—BROBDINGNAG

the habit of arguing that it was really a defense of Anglicanism against other persuasions, but few readers were convinced. Among the decidedly unconvinced was Queen Anne, who saw to it that Swift never got clerical preferment in England; his later assignments in Ireland were a kind of punishment. The episode in "A Voyage to Lilliput" in which Gulliver saves the queen's royal apartment from burning down by spraying a quart or so of urine on it—to her undying disgust—is supposed to have been inspired by Anne's reaction to *A Tale of a Tub.*

Sir William Temple died in 1699, and with the turn of the century Swift began to move into the great world of London letters, politics, and court intrigue. The

three were more or less one and the same: most of the famous writers of the period were also journalists or pamphleteers. Addison, Steele, Congreve, Prior, Gay, Pope, Arbuthnot—Swift came to know them all and to leaven their company as one of the wittiest of the wits. For the next ten years he would be as much a part of London as of Ireland, even though Stella was now established in Dublin at his expense, like a stay-at-home wife. (His letters to her, later collected as the famous *Journal to Stella,* read very much like family letters, full of gossip, reflections on the weather, private jokes, even baby talk.) His London writing—political tracts, humorous poems, some thirty issues of a Tory periodical called the *Examiner*—now began to draw great attention. Most of it was published anonymously, but his style, which was clear and taut, soon became recognizable, and long before he sat down to write *Gulliver's Travels* in the 1720's Swift was famous.

Apparently the first hint of the general shape of *Gulliver* emerged from the Scriblerus Club, a barely organized literary group including Swift, Arbuthnot, Pope, and Oxford. As an amusing joint enterprise they agreed to manufacture the memoirs of one Martinus Scriblerus, whom they described as a savant who "had dipped into every art and science, but injudiciously in each." The short-lived club collapsed in 1714, when Oxford fell from power and the queen died. But when Swift left London he took with him some notes for a treatise on Scriblerus's voyages into certain strange regions of the world. Now dean of St. Patrick's Cathedral in Dublin, the highest office he would ever occupy, he let five or six years go by while he adjusted himself to the unexciting duties of the church and the quiet social life of Dublin and Irish country houses, with Stella always on the scene or waiting in the wings. Then, in about 1720, he began to turn Scriblerus into Gulliver.

Returning to Lilliput and Brobdingnag with some knowledge of Swift's London years, one is more on the lookout for the satirical reefs that lurk beneath the surface calm of his lucid prose. The emperor of Lilliput, convinced that in the Man-Mountain he has the ultimate weapon, sends him to launch a surprise attack on the war fleet of the kingdom of Blefuscu, which Gulliver accomplishes with an éclat that makes Pearl Harbor look like a fiasco. His master is naturally ecstatic when he wades into the royal port of Lilliput, towing the entire enemy fleet behind him like toy boats; but to Gulliver's dismay this is not enough: now His Serene Majesty "seemed to think of nothing less than reducing the whole empire of Blefuscu into a province . . . compelling that people to break the smaller end of their eggs, by which he would remain the sole monarch of the whole world."

Gulliver refuses to be the instrument of this aggression, whereupon the emperor and a junta of ministers make

"The dwarf . . . took me up in both hands, and squeezing my legs together, wedged them into the marrow bone above my waist, where I stuck for some time, and made a very ridiculous figure."
—BROBDINGNAG

plans to get rid of him. The alternatives of burning him to death or shooting him with poisoned arrows are humanely rejected in favor of blinding him ("which his Majesty doth not question you will gratefully and humbly submit to"), this, however, to be followed by gradual starvation; "and immediately upon your death, five or six thousand of his Majesty's subjects might, in two or three days, cut your flesh from your bones, take it away by cart-loads, and bury it in distant parts to prevent infection, leaving the skeleton as a monument of admiration to posterity." This program, of which he is apprised by a friendly minister, has faint appeal for Gulliver, and he defects to Blefuscu, whence he finally makes his way back to that part of the world where man's inhumanity to man is more in proportion to his size.

There is a utopian streak in most satirists, and Swift was no exception. Not content with exposing the absurdity and outrage of things as they are, he mused about how they ought to be; and this occasions some faltering in "A Voyage to Lilliput." He has revealed the Lilliputians as incorrigibly petty, yet when Gulliver describes "their learning, laws, and customs, the manner of educating their children," he begins to sound like Sir Thomas More. In Lilliput fraud is a greater crime than theft; ingratitude is a capital crime; and laws are enforced not only by penalties but by rewards. "In choosing persons for all employments," Gulliver says, "they have more regard to good morals than to great abilities," and nobody can hold public office who disowns belief in a "Divine Providence." Children are educated at supernurseries and allowed to see their parents only twice a year; male and female education is substantially the same—"for their maxim is, that among people of quality, a wife should be always a reasonable and agreeable companion, because she cannot always be young." Like most utopian prescrip-

"Some little unlucky adventures . . . happened in those times when I was left by myself. . . . [I] broke my right shin against the shell of a snail, which I happened to stumble over, as I was walking alone, and thinking on poor England."
—BROBDINGNAG

tions, it is all a bit tiresome, and it tells us more about Swift than about anything else; it is also a jarring interruption.

Swift finds his proper tenor again in "A Voyage to Brobdingnag," where the enormous scale offers grand opportunities for sallies against his favorite target, human pride. Physique takes an awful beating; his description of a wet nurse quieting a squalling baby is enough to cut *Playboy*'s subscription list in half:

I must confess no object ever disgusted me so much as the sight of her monstrous breast, which I cannot tell what to compare with, so as to give the curious reader an idea of its bulk, shape and colour. It stood prominent six foot, and could not be less than sixteen in circumference. The nipple was about half the bigness of my head, and the hue both of that and the dug so varified with spots, pimples and freckles, that nothing could appear more nauseous: for I had a near sight of her, she sitting down the more conveniently to give suck, and I standing on the table. This made me reflect upon the fair skins of our English ladies, who appear so beautiful to us, only because they are of our own size, and their defects not to be seen but through a magnifying glass, where we find by experiment that the smoothest and whitest skins look rough and coarse, and ill coloured.

The incongruity of Gulliver's tiny dimensions and his pretentious claims for European civilization throws the king into a reflective mood:

After I had been a little too copious in talking of my own beloved country, of our trade, and wars by sea and land, of our schisms in religion, and parties in the state; the prejudices of his education prevailed so far, that he could not forbear taking me up in his right hand, and stroking me gently with the other, after an hearty fit of laughing, asked me, whether I were a Whig or a Tory. Then turning to his first minister, who waited behind him with a white staff, near as tall as the mainmast of the *Royal Sovereign*, he observed how contemptible a thing was human grandeur, which could be mimicked by such diminutive insects as I; and yet, said he, I dare engage, these creatures have their titles and distinctions of honour, they contrive little nests and burrows, that they call houses and cities; they make a figure in dress and equipage; they love, they fight, they dispute, they cheat, they betray. And thus he continued on, while my colour came and went several times, with indignation to hear our noble country, the mistress of arts and arms, the scourge of France, the arbitress of Europe, the seat of virtue, piety, honour and truth, the pride and envy of the world, so contemptuously treated.

The *coup de grâce* comes after Gulliver has spent hours giving a detailed account of English government and society. The king, having listened attentively and taken copious notes, makes a long series of pejorative comments, many of which are as embarrassing today as they must have been in 1726—for example, "that certainly we must be a quarrelsome people, or live among very bad neighbours, and that our generals must needs be richer than our kings." He wants to know "what business we had out of our own islands, unless upon the score of trade or treaty, or to defend the coasts with our fleet. Above all, he was amazed to hear me talk of a mercenary standing army in the midst of peace, and among a free people." The king then winds it all up with the famous dictum:

By what I have gathered from your own relation, and the answers I have with much pain wringed and extorted from you, I cannot but conclude the bulk of your natives to be the most pernicious race of little odious vermin that nature ever suffered to crawl upon the surface of the earth.

This was a strange message to be transmitted by the amiable dean of St. Patrick's. By the time *Gulliver* was published, Swift had become one of the most popular men in Ireland, partly for the kind reasonableness with which he administered his parishes, and partly for having championed the cause of Irish nationalism in several devastating pamphlets collectively called *The Drapier's Letters*. But there was more disconcerting stuff to come in the third and fourth parts of *Gulliver's Travels*.

It is usual among critics and professors to disparage "A Voyage to Laputa, Balnibarbi, Glubbdubdrib, Luggnagg and Japan" as the least successful part of Swift's astonishing book. The tale does suffer from not having any bright trick of perspective: the inhabitants of these tongue-twisting countries are of ordinary size and are distinguished only by odd looks and odder behavior. It is also, as the title suggests, a hodgepodge of ridiculous scenes that shift too often.

Yet there are some poignant needles in this haystack, and some amusing ones as well. Scientists, speculative philosophers, theoreticians—these are Swift's whipping boys. In Laputa, an airborne island that seems to be a harbinger of the flying saucer, the gentry are accompanied by servants with blown-up bladders on sticks: "With these bladders they now and then flapped the mouths and ears of those who stood near them. . . . It seems, the minds of these people are so taken up with intense speculations, that they neither can speak, nor attend to the discourses of others, without being roused by some external taction upon the organs of speech and hearing." When Gulliver is ushered before the king, he has to wait about an hour because His Majesty is so deep in thought that his flapper cannot stir him.

At Lagado, in Balnibarbi, the puzzled

traveler visits an Academy of Projectors. Here he observes the aforementioned scientist whose lifework is the analysis of feces; another who aims to extract sunshine from cucumbers; and another whose object is to develop a breed of woolless sheep. A professor of speculative learning, assisted by many students, has contrived a gigantic machine capable of mixing at random all the words in their language. Whenever a few words happen to make sense they are diligently copied down, with the expectation that in the long run by this means, "the most ignorant person at a reasonable charge, and with a little bodily labour, may write books in philosophy, poetry, politics, law, mathematics, and theology, without the least assistance from genius or study."

Well, it does grow tiresome, and on the whole the third book of *Gulliver's Travels* is a letdown. I must attest, however, that I like it better now than I did when I wrote a college paper about it just before World War II. I remember rising to a pinnacle of indignation over Swift's failure to understand the promise of science and technology, which, I felt sure, would eventually solve most if not all human problems. That was before the atomic bomb, smog, dirty water, DDT, and computers. It was also before a famous psychologist at Harvard demonstrated, with a machine rather like the one in the academy at Lagado, that there is no more alliteration in Shakespeare's sonnets than occurs in any random choice of words.

With the last part of *Gulliver*, "A Voyage to the Country of the Houyhnhnms," Swift rediscovers the vein of bold and surprising invention out of which he mined the first two

OVERLEAF:

"*At my alighting I was surrounded by a crowd of people. . . . I observed here and there many in the habit of servants, with a blown bladder fastened like a flail to the end of a short stick, which they carried in their hands. In each bladder was a small quantity of dried pease, or little pebbles. . . . With these bladders they now and then flapped the mouths and ears of those who stood near them, of which practice I could not then conceive the meaning.*"

—LAPUTA

"*These* Yahoos *engendered, and their brood in a short time grew so numerous as to over-run and infest the whole nation. . . . The* Houyhnhnms *to get rid of this evil, made a general hunting, and at last enclosed the whole herd . . . and brought them to such a degree of tameness, as an animal so savage by nature can be capable of acquiring.* —HOUYHNHNMLAND

parts. Suddenly we find ourselves in a land where there appear to be no human beings but Gulliver himself, for the creatures who reign over society here are, of all things, horses. But wait—what are those noisome, naked animals that serve them and run wild across the Houyhnhnm countryside? They are the Yahoos, and they are, in fact, human beings. It is one of Swift's keenest gambits

that the reader discovers this before Gulliver does. He is so taken with disgust at his first sight of them, and learns to despise them so completely upon further observation, that it is only with the most painful reluctance that he finally admits that he is of their kind.

The Yahoos are, to be sure, human beings at their worst—or so we are allowed to think for a while. Physically repulsive, they love filth of every kind and are given to voiding their excrement at the slightest provocation, using it as an expression of displeasure and as a weapon against enemies. They are "cunning, malicious, treacherous, and revengeful"; they are also quarrelsome, greedy, and lecherous. The females are

anything but attractive; they have long, lank hair and habitually go on all fours: "Their dugs hung between their forefeet, and often reached almost to the ground as they walked."

Some critics—notably John Middleton Murry—have remarked that the female Yahoos seem to be selected for Swift's most venomous passages. They are represented as insatiably lascivious, and one incident—wherein Gulliver, bathing naked in a brook, is lubricously assaulted by a raven-haired "girl" of eleven—strikes Murry as, consciously or unconsciously, directed at Stella: "It is impossible to suppress the notion that Swift is engaged in annihilating Stella herself as a sexual being; as it were, cau-

terizing out of his mind, and that retrospectively, as from the moment when he first became conscious of her beauty, the possibility of a sexual relation with her."

This may be going a bit far, yet the focus on sex and excrement in the last book of *Gulliver's Travels* does invite speculation about the libido of the author, whose sexual biography is indeed curious. Swift attracted lovely and intelligent women, and he intensely needed them. He kept poor Stella in limbo from puberty to menopause, and if, as the evidence seems to indicate, he legally married her, there is no hint that the marriage was ever consummated (one of the curious facts of their relationship is that he never permitted her to

see him alone). In London he engaged in a long, semisexual dalliance with another beautiful, and younger, woman, Esther Vanhomrigh ("Vanessa"), who loved him passionately and followed him to Ireland, only to die of tuberculosis and a broken heart when she learned the truth about Swift and Stella.

Meanwhile, back in Houyhnhnmland, the master race are copulating without passion, simply to perpetuate their ineffable species. In addition to the noble dignity with which ordinary horses so often seem to be endowed, they have a list of attributes that would have warmed the heart of Baron Baden-Powell: they are unshakably trustworthy, loyal, helpful, friendly, courteous,

kind, obedient, cheerful, thrifty, brave, clean, and reverent. They are mightily imbued with sweet reason, and although perfectly eloquent in speech, they never argue with one another, since all are naturally in agreement on every question, whether of fact or value.

The juxtaposition between Yahoos and Houyhnhnms is a daring ploy on Swift's part, and he sticks with it bravely. But the suspenders of disbelief, which we have stretched willingly enough in Lilliput and Brobdingnag, finally snap. It is simply too ludicrous to imagine horses building houses, concocting medicine, preparing food, milking cows, cutting hay, and making pottery—and Gulliver's insistence that he saw a mare thread a needle, using "the hollow part between the pastern and the hoof . . . as we do our hands," fails to relieve the spurious air of the whole business. It is a preposterous travesty on what may well be, along with the brain, the greatest achievement of evolution, the human hand. What is worse is that Swift's moral vision seems to have developed a warped lens. The Houyhnhnms are literally too good to be true, and one's heart begins to warm toward the dreadful Yahoos.

But it is too insulting to Swift's intelligence to suppose that he was not well aware of all this. He has concluded by taking us on a voyage that is not just improbable but in large part inconceivable. The Houyhnhnms are an almost abstract projection into a realm of Platonic idealism, while the Yahoos are a *reductio ad absurdum* of human animality. Yet this gives Swift an open field for the kind of satire he likes best, the satire of outrageous hyperbole. Instead of relaying to his master a sober précis of European morals and manners, as he did for the king of Brobdingnag, Gulliver pours out a catalogue of paralyzing exaggerations, all the while protesting that, if anything, he is understating the facts: "In what I said of my countrymen, I extenuated their faults as much as I durst . . . and upon every article gave as favourable a turn as the matter would bear."

Favorable! Here are lawyers: "A society of men among us, bred up from their youth in the art of proving by words multiplied for the purpose, that white is black, and black is white, according as they are paid. To this society all the rest of the people are slaves."

And judges: "Picked out from the most dexterous lawyers, who are grown old or lazy, and having been biassed all their lives against truth and equity, are under . . . a fatal necessity of favouring fraud, perjury, and oppression."

Here are doctors: "One great excellency in this tribe is their skill at prognostics, wherein they seldom fail; their predictions in real diseases, when they rise to any degree of malignity, generally

portending death, which is always in their power, when recovery is not: and therefore, upon any unexpected signs of amendment, after they have pronounced their sentence, rather than be accused as false prophets, they know how to approve their sagacity to the world by a seasonable dose."

And here is the chief executive: "A creature wholly exempt from joy and grief, love and hatred, pity and anger; at least [making] use of no other passions but a violent desire of wealth, power, and titles; that he applies his words to all uses, except to the indication of his mind; that he never tells a truth, but with an intent that you should take it for a lie; nor a lie, but with a design that you should take it for a truth. . . . The worst mark you can receive is a promise, especially when it is confirmed with an oath; after which every wise man retires, and gives over all hopes."

It is laughable, of course—yet our laughter has a hollow ring, for Swift's hyperbole is often squirmishly near the truth. Much depends on time, place, and circumstance. In the year. of our Lord 1976, for example, Gulliver's account of power politics is not so funny: "If a prince sends forces into a nation, where the people are poor and ignorant, he may lawfully put half of them to death, and make slaves of the rest, in order to civilize and reduce them from their barbarous way of living." And his definition of a soldier raises haunting memories: "A *Yahoo* hired to kill in cold blood as many of his own species . . . as possibly he can."

Swift knew very well what he was about, and he must have realized that the last part of *Gulliver's Travels* would repel thousands of readers and open himself to charges of misanthropy. The crowning insult comes when Gulliver's master, pondering what he has heard, concludes that civilized men are *worse* than Yahoos, having corrupted their natural vices by misapplication of the small amount of reason they have accidentally acquired. It is Dean Swift's ultimate joke. He does, of course, detest mankind: no satirist worth his salt does

"*I . . . went down softly into the stream. It happened that a young female Yahoo, standing behind a bank, saw the whole proceeding, and inflamed by desire . . . came running with all speed, and leaped into the water. . . . I was never in my life so terribly frightened. . . . She embraced me after a most fulsome manner; I roared as loud as I could.*"
—HOUYHNHNMLAND

not. He was a worldly man despite his clerical collar, and he had unblinkingly observed human behavior for fifty years, during many of which his native acidity was exacerbated by deafness and vertigo caused by a lesion of the inner ear. Yet a clergyman in his late fifties does not labor for several years over a satire aimed at the general reading public without a stubborn hope that men and women may be, after all, stung, lashed, and jabbed into better sense.

Gulliver's Travels was an immediate success when it was published in 1726. Everyone knew who the anonymous author was: Swift's position in the literary world was well-established in his own lifetime. It was translated quickly into French: "The more I read your works," Voltaire wrote Swift, "the less I am satisfied with my own." *Candide* was still a quarter of a century in the future; but if the most brilliant prose satire in French owes one thing to the most brilliant prose satire in English, it is Voltaire's awareness of how profoundly entertaining such a work could be.

Dean Swift died in 1745, having outlived Stella, Vanessa, and his wit—he was half mad during his last few years. He was buried in his own cathedral under an epitaph he wrote himself:

The body of Jonathan Swift . . . Dean of this Cathedral, is buried here, where fierce indignation no longer can lacerate his heart. Go, traveller, and imitate if you can one who did his best to champion freedom.

It was, above all, freedom from irrationality that Swift championed, and in the end the shafts of light that *Gulliver's Travels* throws on the abuse of human reason are what justify its position among the world's towering classics.

E. M. Halliday, a mere 6 feet 2 inches, is editor of American Heritage *magazine.*

"Are you telling them that it is an utterly useless war?"

Those who do not learn from the mistakes of the past are condemned not merely to repeat them but also, it would seem, to have their lessons recur in increasingly harsh and brutal—ultimately, perhaps, fatal—form. Such, in any case, is one impression left by a recent book that has been deservedly praised, Phillip Knightley's *The First Casualty*, a history of war reporting from the Crimea to Vietnam, published last fall by Harcourt Brace Jovanovich.

Knightley is concerned with whether the proper role of the war correspondent is to try to tell the truth or, as has more often been the case, to serve as cheerleader for one side or another. His method is a series of case studies—brisk narratives of wars and battles, as they have been reported and as they truly occurred. The tension that he develops between the newspaper stories and the truth behind the stories is completely absorbing, and at times excruciating. And his final conclusion is dismaying: war reporting has generally been so poor "that you were very lucky indeed reading your paper back home to have any idea of what was happening."

Knightley surveys war correspondents from William Howard Russell, a reporter on the Crimean War for the London *Times* and the first of the professional war correspondents (otherwise reckoned "the miserable parent of a luckless tribe"), through Winston Churchill, Evelyn Waugh (who was sacked for sending a cable back home in untranslatable "cablese Latin"), Ernest Hemingway (who invented dialogue for his stories), to such contemporary Americans as David Halberstam of the *New York Times*.

He concludes, with Senator Hiram Johnson, that "the first casualty when war comes is truth," and his book should make us all more careful and skeptical newspaper readers.

Knightley is well qualified to write such a book. He is a journalist with some thirty years' experience, a reporter for the London *Sunday Times*, co-author of *The Philby Conspiracy* and *The Secret Lives of Lawrence of Arabia*, and a lively writer with a sharp eye. His book as a whole is fascinating and illuminating, but I am especially seized by his account of the reporting

Korea, 1950: U.S. Marines slog through the snow near Koto-ri.

DEFENSE DEPARTMENT PHOTO (MARINE CORPS)

of the Korean War, which was, as one reporter called it, "a prep school for Vietnam."

"Are you correspondents telling the people back home the truth?" one young lieutenant asked Marguerite Higgins of the New York *Herald Tribune*. "Are you telling them that out of one platoon of twenty men, we have three left? Are you telling them that we have nothing to fight with, and that it is an utterly useless war?"

In the beginning of the war the correspondents did at least report the terrible punishment that green United Nations troops were taking at the hands of a better army. But they were not raising questions of the utility of the war, or any of the larger questions

that clamored for attention behind the front lines. Nor did battle-front reportage rise to a higher standard as the war continued. General MacArthur's headquarters sent out word that most of the journalists who reported the plain truth were "giving aid and comfort to the enemy."

Finally, of course, military censorship was imposed. "The new instructions," Knightley writes, "included the usual limitations on matters involving military security, but . . . it was now forbidden to make any criticism of the allied conduct of the war or 'any derogatory comments' about United Nations troops or commanders, quite unprecedented restrictions. Clearly, from now on the war was going to be reported only the way the military wanted it to be. There were protests. The *London Daily Dispatch* said censorship was now so tight that it was no longer officially possible to say anything about [UN] troops other than that they were in Korea."

It would have been possible for all the war correspondents simply to withdraw from Korea, and for newspapers to print nothing but military handouts labeled as such. Somehow such a strategic withdrawal never occurs to journalists—a fact that can hardly be wondered at. The best of them stay on, hoping they can uncover —and get past the censors— something worthwhile. They rarely did in Korea, and, in any event, as Knightley writes, "there is evidence that, even without the new censorship, a backlash had begun against the early critical reporting of the war, a feeling that it was time to 'get on side' and stop helping the Reds." So the copy poured out—about amphibious landings, about patrols, snipers, and land mines.

The battle-front correspondents, Knightley says, "wrote the usual 'I-was-there' copy, especially Marguerite Higgins and [Homer] Bigart, who took chances that others rejected and spurred each other on in a private competition to get top billing on the *Herald Tribune*'s front page. 'This correspondent was one of three reporters who saw the action,' wrote Bigart, 'and the only newsman to get out alive.'" In the middle of the Inchon landing, according to James Cameron of the *Picture Post*, "if you can conceive of such a thing, there was a wandering boat, marked in great letters PRESS, full of agitated and contending correspondents, all trying to appear insistently determined to land in Wave One, while contriving desperately to be found in Wave Fifty."

"Trying to report the war," Knightley writes, "now became close to a farce. The United States Air Force began issuing bulletins in which pilots gave the figures of enemy killed down to the last man. Soon MacArthur's intelligence officers followed suit, and from previously not having known the enemy's strength to within 100,000 or 200,000, they now claimed to know the numbers of Chinese involved down to single figures." At one point, the "'Chinese hordes' were swollen to nearly a million in a few days, though everywhere out of contact. The briefings finally ended when Michael Davidson of the *Observer* asked, with deceptive seriousness, 'Will you tell us how many Chinese battalions go to a horde, or vice-versa?'"

Still, such questions as these are battle-front questions, and as important as they are, they do not address such essential issues as the utility of the war itself, or even what sort of ally America had embraced in Syngman Rhee and his regime. "The police," Knightley observes, "who had been trained by the Japanese, were heavily involved in the black market. . . . It was not unknown for South Korean conscripts to die of starvation in military camps because corrupt officers

had profiteered on food supplies. There had been 14,000 political prisoners in jail awaiting trial at the outbreak of the war. Executions for political reasons began when Seoul was recaptured by the allies." Among those shot were women and children.

Some journalists reported such things—and their editors back home declined to print the reports. Edward R. Murrow recorded a critical report on the war, which CBS decided not to use. I. F. Stone's *The Hidden History of the Korean War*, which he wanted to have published first in Great Britain, was submitted to twenty-eight publishers before the Monthly Review Press accepted it. Not a single major American newspaper opposed the war or consistently probed the essential questions it raised. Nor did anyone comment much on the racism of the war, though Reginald Thompson did write that the Americans "never spoke of the enemy as though they were people, but as one might speak of apes. If they remarked a dead Korean body . . . it was simply 'dead Gook' or 'good Gook.'" The same racism would return to haunt Vietnam.

In the end, few people even understood what was happening in the peace talks. On June 2, 1951, Secretary of State Dean Acheson announced that the United States would accept a cease-fire based on the 38th parallel. The North Koreans had consistently maintained that they had been invaded by the South, so presumably the 38th parallel cease-fire line was also acceptable to them. Why, then, was there no agreement? Knightley says:

While the United Nations was refusing to discuss a cease-fire at the thirty-eighth parallel and demanding one thirty-two miles to the north instead, the correspondents were told that it was the North Koreans who were refusing to accept the thirty-eighth parallel. A map of the precise truce-line positions the United Nations was demanding, which was displayed in the allied press tent, turned out to be faked, and though the North Korean and Chinese delegates proposed a demarcation line along the exact existing battle line, a settlement acceptable to world opinion, the

briefing officers flatly denied that any such proposals had ever been made.

The truth of these shenanigans was reported by Wilfred Burchett, who wrote for *Ce Soir*, and Alan Winnington, who wrote for the London *Daily Worker*. Both Burchett and Winnington were friendly with the North Korean–Chinese delegation, and other journalists were discouraged from relying on them as secondhand sources. General Matthew B. Ridgway issued a memorandum on the subject: "The UN Command view with growing apprehension the practice of some reporters of excessive social consorting, including the drinking of alcoholic beverages, with communist journalists." Lamentably, however, readers of *Ce Soir* and the *Daily Worker* were getting more reliable reports of the negotiations than most Americans.

Yet another question was ignored at the time of the Korean War, and still is today: Was it necessary? "Korea has been a blessing," said General James A. Van Fleet. "There had to be a Korea either here or some place in the world." That is, if the United States had not fought in Korea, it might have had to fight in, say, Vietnam.

Since the end of the Vietnam war, the American press has been generally self-congratulatory or, on occasion, apologetic about the power it holds and directs so devastatingly against politicians and policies. One wonders what the press is so apologetic about. It was not notably on the *qui vive* at the beginning of the Vietnam war, nor were the American people. The lessons of Korea had to be taught all over again. It was not enough in Korea to have casualties of three hundred thousand allied soldiers and two million civilians, and to leave one hundred thousand children orphaned. The lessons had to be taught again, and more brutally: specific lessons about getting involved in wars, choosing allies, surrendering great powers to presidents, and one general lesson—that the press and the people have a right, and duty, to be much tougher on their public servants. Must we be taught again?

How the Three-Piece Suit and the Modern World Began

By G. BRUCE BOYER

In 1660 Charles II was restored to his throne and came home from what he called his "travels" in France. He had, in those bitter years abroad, adopted many French fashions, but now he was back in England, in his own court. On October 8, 1666, Samuel Pepys heard that King Charles had made an unprecedented decision:

The King hath yesterday in council declared his resolution of setting a fashion for clothes, which he will never alter. It will be a vest, I know not well how. But it is to teach the nobility thrift, and will do good.

Charles, who was wiser than his biographers generally concede, used this excuse for setting the new fashion. However, the marquis of Halifax suggested a deeper motivation for the change:

About this time a general humour, in opposition to France, had made us throw off their fashion, and put on vests, that we might look more like a distinct people, and not be under the servility of imitation. . . .

Whether the king was in the forefront of this movement or merely caught the blowing wind of popular resentment in his sail is not clear. We do know that the new style of dress became popular immediately. Pepys was at Whitehall the following Saturday, October 13, and found the king's brother, the duke of York, "just come in from hunting."

So I stood and saw him dress himself and try on his Vest, which is the King's new fashion, and will be in it for good and all on Monday next, the whole Court: it is a fashion the King says he will never change.

And so, on that memorable Monday—October 15, 1666—Pepys went to Westminster Hall to see the king in his new finery:

This day the King begins to put on his Vest, and I did see several persons of the House of Lords, and Commons too, great courtiers, who are in it—being a long Cassocke close to the body, of black cloth and pinked [i.e., slashed] with white silk under it, and a coat over it, and the legs ruffled with black riband like a pigeon's leg—and upon the whole, I wish the King may keep it, for it is a very fine and handsome garment.

Three days later, John Evelyn reported that "divers courtiers and gentlemen gave his Majesty gold by way of wager that he would not persist in this resolution." They would have lost the bet, for the king continued to wear his new costume, and the modern three-piece suit—coat, vest, and trousers— was regally on its way.

On October 17, however, Pepys had heard that Charles was already beginning to modify his new costume:

The Court is all full of Vests; only my Lord St. Albans not pinked, but plain black—and they say the King says the pinking upon white makes them look too much like magpyes, and therefore hath bespoke one of plain velvet.

Pepys himself was quick to perceive that the style had caught on (it being rather difficult to resist a royal imprimatur) and immediately ordered a suit in the new style. It was delivered to him on November 4, a Sunday:

Comes my Taylor's man in the morning and brings my vest home, and coat to wear with it, and belt and silver-hilted sword. So I rose and dressed myself, and I like myself mightily in it, and so doth my wife. Then being dressed to church.

In the same entry he relates a liability of the new costume:

And after dinner to the waterside, and so, it being very cold, to White-hall, and was mighty fearfull of an ague (my vest being new and thin, and the Coate cut not to meet before upon my breast).

Modishness, he might have observed, is not necessarily allied with comfort. But Pepys put on the new style with the rest of London, and even learned that Lord Halifax was probably right about the political reason for the change:

I to my office, where very late and did much business, and then home, and there find Mr. Batelier [who] tells me the news how the King of France hath, in defiance to the King of England, caused all his footmen to be put into Vests . . . which, if true, is the greatest indignity ever done by one prince to another. . . . This makes me mighty merry, it being an ingenious kind of affront; but yet makes me angry to see that the King of England is become so little. . . .

If Louis did concoct this glorious prank, and there is some evidence that he did, it soon backfired. By the turn of the century all Europe was wearing the new clothing of the English court.

October 8, 1666, marks, therefore, a turning point in social history. From that day on, the rigid formality of court dress was doomed, and the swing toward sartorial democracy had begun —a process initiated, ironically, by a restored monarch. As Geoffrey Squire so aptly points out in *Dress and Society*, "when men gave up doublet and hose in favour of coat, waistcoat and breeches they had taken an irreversible step towards the modern world, in which technology, science and industry take precedence over instinct, intuition and craftsmanship."

Charles II models a trio of men's suits: a doublet and breeches from the time of James I; the new mode introduced in 1666; and a stylish modern example of the three-piecer.